The **Mormon Role** *in the* **Settlement** *of the* **West**

Charles
Redd
Monographs
in Western
History No. 9

The *Mormon Role* in the Settlement of the West

Richard H. Jackson, Editor

Brigham Young University Press

*The Charles Redd Monographs in Western
History are made possible by a grant from
Charles Redd. This grant served as the basis
for the establishment of the Charles Redd
Grant for Western Studies at Brigham Young
University.*

Center editor: Thomas G. Alexander
Press editor: Howard A. Christy

International Standard Book Number: 0-8425-1321-3
Library of Congress Catalog Card Number: 78-24728

Brigham Young University Press, Provo, Utah 84602
© 1978 by Brigham Young University Press. All rights reserved

Printed in the United States of America

Additional copies of this monograph or other numbers in this series may be
purchased by writing to Business Office, 205 University Press Building,
Brigham Young University, Provo, Utah 84602

78 850p 34451

Contents

Introduction

Almost everyone in the United States is familiar with the broad outline of the Mormon role in settling the western United States. The drama associated with Brigham Young and the epic journey of the Mormons to the Rocky Mountains has inspired numerous articles and books. The trying years of struggle as the Saints persevered in their attempts to transform the desert has provided material for novelists, movie makers, and scholars. It might seem presumptuous, therefore, to offer yet another work dealing with the Mormons and the West. In recent years, however, there has been a renewed interest as scholars have attempted to recreate and reassess the Mormon settlement in the West and the subsequent development of a unique people in a unique place. The papers in this volume represent original studies which address a number of central questions concerning the Mormon role in occupation of the land. Central to the papers included in this volume is an attempt to probe into the actual occurrences and to avoid common stereotypes regarding the Mormon role in the settlement of the West. Taken as a whole, the articles provide a stimulating insight into the Mormon experience which should leave the reader with an entirely new viewpoint and encourage further research to answer the unanswered questions.

The journey to Salt Lake by converts to Mormonism is explored by Richard Jackson. Central to any celebration of the entry of Brigham Young into the Salt Lake Valley on July 24, 1847, are orations on the tremendous suffering of the Mormon pioneers who crossed the plains between 1847 and 1869. Listeners are informed that the Saints faced untold perils in crossing great deserts to Utah. Dr. Jackson examines the pioneer journey through analysis of the diaries of those who participated in it and suggests that for the typical migrant the journey may not have been as arduous as popularly conceived.

The high degree of Mormon organization coupled with experienced leaders minimized hardships on the overland trip in all but a few years. Although still subject to illness and accident, traveling across the plains was little different from other travel in the pre-railroad era—slow, uncomfortable, and tedious. Since they approached the trip across the plains with familiarity with walking or wagon travel, the migrants accepted it as a natural part of travel.

Few diarists complained about the difficulty of the trip, and to most the one-way journey to their new home was a highlight of their lives. Diarists responded like typical tourists, commenting on scenic views, curiosities, and acquaintances in the camp. Even after a twenty-five-mile hike during the day, entire camps were willing to walk additional miles to see some landmark along the trail.

The journey of some 60,000 people across the plains under Mormon supervision was a great achievement, but that achievement, according to Jackson, centered on its accomplishment by average individuals. The mere fact that thousands of people of all ages were willing to make the journey for their faith is a miracle in itself. The Mormon settlers of the American West were not supermen, only ordinary individuals who accomplished the seemingly impossible because of their faith and persistence. Viewed in this light, Jackson suggests, the trip across the plains was more important as a unifier of the Saints than as a trial by hardship.

The exploration of their new home by the Saints has never been adequately documented because exploration was only incidental to settlement and records of most explorations were never published. Melvin Smith discusses the Mormon experience in exploring one portion of the Colorado River area incidental to Mormon attempts to develop navigation on the river. Although the focus of the paper is a limited area along the lower Colorado River, the events affecting Mormon exploration are related to broader events and policies affecting the Mormon leaders and their decisions.

Mormon efforts to settle in the arid region of southwestern Utah and Nevada along tributaries to the Colorado River were heroic. Since the area was only marginally habitable at best, supreme effort was required to enable the settlers to create a viable community. Central to successful settlement was accessibility, and the Colorado seemed to provide an alternative to the tortuous and tedious overland journey. Dr. Smith analyzes the explorers of the lower Colorado, including both Mormon and non-Mormon exploring parties. Early Mormon explorations of the area were by missionaries to the Indians, but the coming of the 1860's and the Civil War fostered greater interest in the Colorado's possibilities. Establishment of the Deseret Mercantile Association in 1864 culminated in the construction of Call's Landing on the Colorado in 1865. The fascinating story of the abandonment of the warehouse by the Mormons is examined by Smith, who hypothesizes on the underlying premise of the Mormon exploration in the lower Colorado and colonization attempts in general. The lower Colorado exploration becomes a microcosm in which Mormon colonization efforts in the west are analyzed. Dr. Smith's study suggests that in the exploration of the lower Colorado and elsewhere the Mormon leaders suffered not only from incomplete information, but also from information colored by the wishful thinking of Mormon missionaries, explorers, the settlers, and the leaders themselves.

Lynn Rosenvall examines an aspect of Mormon colonization of the West rarely discussed and provides an analysis of which communities failed and why they did so. Given the harsh environmental setting of the West, it was inevitable that some settlements would not be successful. This factor was compounded by the prevailing antagonistic attitudes the Mormons encountered in their settlement efforts in the midwest and west. In combination, the physical environment and events in the broader American society caused the failure of less than 15 percent of settlements established by the Saints. The success ratio of over 80 percent is a testimonial to the perseverance of the settlers as they refused to abandon marginal locations.

Abandonment of Mormon settlements came in response to a variety of factors. Indian conflicts, revolutions as in Mexico, border changes as in the Muddy settlements of Nevada, and public sentiment against polygamy all forced settlers to temporarily or permanently abandon their homes. Ironically, Dr. Rosenvall points out that the drought associated with the West and semiarid West did not cause the demise of many communities, but abandonment came rather because of flooding which destroyed dams and precious farm land. A host of other environmental factors caused community abandonment, but abandonment came only after prolonged struggle to overcome the problems of the area. Once committed to a location, the Mormons were extremely reluctant to abandon it; and as Professor Rosenvall points out, those which were abandoned represented the most marginal locations. Dr. Rosenvall's concise analysis of a topic rarely studied will no doubt become the reference standard for study of abandoned Mormon communities.

Alan Grey uses comparative analysis to illustrate that much of the claim of uniqueness commonly made for the Mormon experience represents more a lack of analysis of broader events contemporary with the Mormons. Using the example of the settlement of Christchurch, New Zealand, Dr. Grey discusses the similarities and differences between it and the Mormon settlements and concludes that while widely separated in space, they are quite close in character.

The milieu in which both developed had its origin in the expansion of western Europe in the fifteenth and sixteenth centuries. Thus, although the Mormons represented the egalitarian utopias developed in early nineteenth century America and the New Zealand settlement envisioned not the establishment of a new order but reestablishment of a perceived older class-oriented society, both followed similar processes. In the case of the Mormons, they established communities to ensure provision of education and other amenities for the Saints. In the case of Christchurch, the developers also established communities with the goal of providing amenities, including religion. From this similarity of purpose Dr. Grey proceeds to examine other aspects of the two settlements to illustrate his thesis. The fact that the Mormon experience in settlement was less unique than often believed should come as no surprise. The forces and events which affected the Mormons and facilitated their successful colonization fostered similar activity among other groups of west European background. Although Dr. Grey examines only one example, others could be cited to further indicate the general conformity of the Mormon settlement activity to the events transpiring elsewhere.

The settlements established by the Mormons created a unique landscape in western America. Charles Peterson, in a provocative paper, analyzes the development of the agricultural systems associated with Mormon settlement and details the development of the Mormon landscape. Central to this landscape, of course, was the village with its large lots devoted to mini-farms. Surrounding the village were larger fields to which the settlers commuted, but initially there were few ranches or independent farmsteads occupied by their owners. As a result, the villages emerged as the dominant feature of the landscape and received the attention of numerous descriptive narratives of the era even though the Mormon impact on the landscape extended beyond the confines of the community.

This impact can be seen even today in the relatively fragmented nature of the land around the Mormon village caused by fencing. These fences represent the original subdivision of the farming lands which ensured that all settlers had access to the agricultural resource base of the area. Beyond the cultivated lands, the Mormon impact remains in the form of the overgrazing associated with the Mormon development of sheep and cattle production using the nonarable lands in the more rugged mountains and plateaus surrounding their settlements. Erosion associated with this overgrazing sculpted the landscape permanently.

Since initially the Mormons had not owned property, the extension of the Homestead Act to Utah resulted in a superimposition of quarter sections and isolated farmsteads over the existing village morphology. With the passage of time and the growth of population in Utah, large-scale reclamation projects were developed and additional lands were opened to irrigation and settlement, often in the form of dispersed farmsteads or string villages rather than nucleated Mormon villages.

Beyond the irrigated lands in the marginal areas of Utah, settlement occurred at a later date and under different economic conditions introducing other variants into the Mormon landscape. The development of dry farming, which affected large areas of Utah, created a landscape of isolated farmsteads; and development of ranching land led to the development of small towns to service them. The coming of the railroad added another element in the form of railroad towns such as Corinne. All of these elements—village, homestead, and dispersed farmstead—represented the attempts of the Mormon settlers to occupy the land of their new Zion in the West. In more recent years these elements have faced extinction as the result of pressures causing urbanization of America, but relics remain of each to create a distinctive Mormon landscape.

Wayne Wahlquist examines the population of Utah in an insightful article that examines official census statistics and compares them with the population figures estimated by Utah officials, Mormon and non-Mormon. Great disparities exist in all of the accounts, and Dr. Wahlquist arrives at an independent figure based on conventional statistical analysis of migration and birth and death rates among the population. His conclusions about the actual population of Utah Territory between 1850 and 1870 provide a base line against which future analysis of migration and population growth in Utah will be measured.

Not content with providing the gross population figures for the entire territory, Wahlquist provides the reader data on the population characteristics of individual communities. The uniformity of age and sex characteristics in the Mormon communities could be anticipated from the Mormon colonization program. More surprising is the extremely high proportion of children found in the Mormon towns. With nearly 50 percent of each Mormon town composed of children, it is little wonder that the communities grew rapidly.

Migrants were an important part of Utah's growth; but unlike other areas of the United States, in Utah the migrants (primarily Mormons) tended to be diffused rather evenly throughout the communities, with concentration of people of similar nationalities the exception rather than the rule. The process by which new migrants arrived and they and their children became assimilated into a unique Mormon culture is an important feature of the colonization of the West by the Mormons.

The expansion of the Mormon people beyond the settlements of the Wasatch Front can be viewed as a final, and ongoing, chapter of the Mormon role in settling the West. Using a series of maps, Lowell Bennion and Dean Louder examine the diffusion of Mormons across America through time, and they suggest a region of Mormon dominance. They begin their analysis of Mormon distribution in 1860 by showing those counties with LDS wards at that time, and then map the expansion of wards to other counties for succeeding decades. The distribution of Mormon congregations by counties illustrates the expansion of the Church during the period of colonization. By 1890 the colonizing period was nearly at an end and the growth of the Church came from intensification of the number of wards within the existing areas of settlement. This trend continued until the end of World War I, when new expansion occurred as Mormons from the agrarian settlements of the Intermountain West began migrating to California. This migration to the West Coast was slow prior to World War II, but wards and stakes were organized in the West Coast states as well as in the Chicago, Milwaukee, and New York areas by 1940.

The period following World War II was one of rapid growth in the non-Utah regions of the U.S., and by 1975 wards had been established in nearly every state in the union. Nevertheless, Utah continues to have the greatest Church membership found in any individual state. Because of the continued concentration of membership in Utah and the West, it is possible to define an area of Mormon dominance, a Mormon cultural region. Bennion and Louder conclude that in terms of membership distribution the Mormons remain a western, and predominantly intermountain, church. Although members of the Church are diffused worldwide, the areas of Mormon dominance reflect the original settlement pattern of the Saints.

Richard H. Jackson

The Overland Journey to Zion

Richard H. Jackson

The Perilous Journey

The overland journey to Utah by Mormon migrants in the pre-railroad years is an important part of the Mormon experience in settling the West. The perils of the journey have been recounted in statements by Mormon leaders, in published and unpublished histories, and in folklore. The typical account of the trip across the plains suggests that it was a journey of extreme hardships and suffering. "Our toilsome journey ... over a desert for upwards of a thousand miles" involved difficulties "such as are unparalleled in the history of mankind," according to George A. Smith in 1860.[1] With the passage of time the "unparalleled" journey of the migrants expanded to an even greater difficulty as the "desert" grew ever more forbidding. "It was the faith and hope that induced the pioneers ... to face savages and to penetrate through a trackless, howling desert."[2] The "trackless, howling desert" described in the 1870s account presented such hardships to the migrants that the accomplishment of the Mormons in getting safely to Utah was described as "one of the greatest miracles since Moses passed over the Red Sea."[3]

Just as the plains crossed by the Mormons had been transformed into deserts through time, so the magnitude of the accomplishment in crossing them grew commensurately. The words of one Mormon leader, "I do not believe that the history of the world records as great a miracle,"[4] state succinctly the extent of this achievement. When compared to the Mormon migration, that of Moses and the Israelites paled. The Mormon journey "was one of the greatest achievements over natural obstacles ever accomplished upon earth.... It is of such a character that the leading of Israel through the wilderness bears no comparison."[5]

Certainly some of the handcart companies suffered drastically, and in some years cholera epidemics caused high death rates among the migrants; but these were the exception rather than the rule. The suffering of the handcart pioneers was the result of a combination of poor judgment by Franklin D. Richards and an early winter, and the cholera epidemics struck throughout the United States in 1849 and 1866. For the typical Mormon migrant, however, the journey seems to have been rather routine.

The Pleasure Trip

After the initial groups of 1847, the migrant companies had as leaders men who had crossed the plains at least once, and in many cases several times. Each year men and wagons were sent out to meet the migrants at Winter Quarters. These guides had made the west-east journey only weeks prior to their east-west trip, and were knowledgeable concerning conditions along the trail. Moreover, traveling by foot or by animal-drawn vehicle was the norm at the time. Only the length of the journey through uninhabited areas was unique. The high degree of organization among the Mormons and relative ease of travel caused diarists to describe their journey not as a trip across a "trackless, howling desert," but as a rather enjoyable event. "The journey across the plains is a very slow process of traveling, but with our order it is rendered as easy as possible," reported a young male migrant of 1854.[6] The description of a female migrant of 1862 summarizes the typical reaction to the trip to Utah:

I never enjoyed better health in my life than while crossing the plains and up to the present time: not the least cause for complaint. We arrived in G.S.L. City on September 23rd, having left Florence[7] on June 23rd, being exactly two months, by the day of the month, in crossing the plains, the quickest trip ever known to have been made with ox-teams. We had a good captain in Captain Homer Duncan, whose train I came in; good teamsters and a good time of it altogether; no accidents of any account; no waggons upset, and the best of time with the cattle. I enjoyed myself very much while travelling, each day bringing its own trials, its pleasures and excitements. The journey to me was a source of much enjoyment and pleasure.[8]

Within a few years after the founding of Salt Lake City, even non-Mormon accounts were describing the ease and efficiency of the Mormon trip across the plains. In 1855 the *New York Tribune* pointed out the safety of the trip under Mormon guidance.

In every seaport of any consequence in this country and in Europe, emigration agents are located to give information to the inquiring, and to aid those who desire to go to Utah, and arrange for their safe and speedy transportation to that distant country. All along the line of travel, too, other agents are waiting with the necessary supplies for the journey, and under the auspices of Mormonism the great land journey across the plains is now almost as safe as a journey from New York to Albany.[9]

Organization for the Journey

The relative ease of the Mormon emigrants' journey was the result of the strict degree of organization followed by each company. On January 14, 1847, Brigham Young announced the pattern which was to be followed by all emigrant companies:

Let all the people of the Church of Jesus Christ of Latter-day Saints, and those who journey with them, be organized into companies, with a covenant and promise to keep all the commandments and statutes of the Lord our God.

Let the Companies be organized with captains of hundreds, captains of fifties, and captains of tens . . . .

Let each company provide themselves with all the teams, wagons, provisions, clothing and other necessaries for the journey.[10]

A typical group of ten heads of families and their possessions is given by group captain Norton Jacob. His group of ten familes consisted of 13 men, 9 women, and 37 children. Their possessions consisted of 16 wagons, 36 yoke of oxen, 29 mules, 10 horses, 214 bushels of flour, 220 bushels of cornmeal, 10 bushels of corn, 50 pounds of meat, 25 dollars in cash, and miscellaneous items such as a chest of joiner's tools, 33 plows, axes, and saws.[11] (See Table 1 for examples of the constituents of five companies of hundreds.)

Once the journey commenced, emigrants were expected to adhere to the rules of their company. The following is the instruction of Brigham Young to the pioneer company in regard to the order of the camp. Other companies had rules which differed only slightly from these.

At 5:00 in the morning the bugle is to be sounded as a signal for every man to arise and attend prayers before he leaves his wagon. Then cooking, eating, feeding teams, etc., till seven o'clock, at which time the camp is to move at the sound of the bugle. Each teamster to keep beside his team, with his loaded gun in his hands or in his wagon where he can get it in a moment. The extra men, each to walk opposite his wagon with his loaded gun on his shoulder, and no man to be permitted to leave his wagon unless he obtains permission from his officer. In case of an attack from Indians or hostile appearances, the wagons to travel in double file. The order of encampment to be a circle with the mouth of the wagon to the outside, and the horses and stock tied inside the circle. At 8:30 p.m. the bugle to be sounded again at which time all to have prayers in their wagons and to retire to rest by nine o'clock.[12]

The leaders pointed out that these rules applied to all, and "if there was any along who did not like to obey the necessary rules of the camp without murmering, to turn back now."[13]

The daily activities associated with camp organization were described by most diarists. Typical is the following account of Ellen Hallett in a letter to her parents in England in 1862.

We enjoyed the journey much. We used to get up in the morning, often when the moon and stars were shining, and get our breakfast, take down our tents and go up to the front of camp to prayers, and then off on the road. We stopped for dinner sometimes one, sometimes two hours, and then off again, stopping to camp at sun-down, perhaps a little sooner or a little later; this depending on our being near to water. We had plenty of good fodder all the way; and plenty of wood, with the exception of one part of the way where we gathered 'buffalo chips'. When night came we were generally tired but not too much so to enjoy the dance and song.[14]

An Overview of the Journey

The journey to Salt Lake City was mentally divided by the Mormon travelers into two parts. The first part of some five hundred miles to Fort Laramie was viewed as "plains." "The first 500 miles of the journey is called the plains, and truly so called. We traveled about that distance, in nearly a straight line, by one river, the Platte."[15] The remainder of the journey was through country viewed as hilly and mountainous. "We arrived at Fort John [Laramie] on 1st June, and

TABLE 1

ORGANIZATION OF PIONEER COMPANIES[a]

Companies of hundreds	Allen Taylor	Lorenzo Snow	William G. Perkins	Zera Pulsipher	Heber C. Kimball[b]	TOTALS
Waggons	190	99	57	51	226	623
Souls	597	321	155	156	662	1891
Horses	30	20	14	10	57	131
Mules	16	3	0	0	25	44
Oxen	615	308	191	161	737	2012
Cows	316	188	99	96	284	983
Loose cattle	63	38	34	49	150	334
Sheep	134	139	97	41	243	654
Pigs	66	25	28	22	96	237
Chickens	282	158	94	71	299	904
Cats	19	10	3	5	17	54
Dogs	31	26	12	13	52	134
Goats	3	0	0	0	0	3
Geese	8	0	0	2	0	10
Bee hives	0	0	2	0	3	5
Doves	6	2	0	0	3	11
Squirrels	0	0	0	0	1	1
Ducks	0	0	0	0	5	5

[a]*Millennial Star* 10(1848):314.

[b]300 families.

then commenced our journey over hills and mountains. No person can help noticing the sudden transition from level and sandy roads to the mountain roads."[16]

The trip, while somewhat long and monotonous, was invariably viewed in favorable terms. One emigrant wrote to her parents in Leeds, England, that the journey to her "was a source of much enjoyment and pleasure. The varied scenery, the aspect of the country, so new to me and different from anything I had ever seen, ... combined to make the time pass swiftly along."[17] Others pointed out, however, that in traveling by ox team there was "less or more of monotony."[18] Nevertheless, such monotony was somewhat relieved by "the happy, cheerful spirit which prevailed in our midst."[19]

Even the seemingly endless miles the emigrants walked were found to be acceptable. One emigrant, reporting that the company walked ten to fifteen miles a day at the start and twenty to twenty-five daily

TABLE 2

A RECORD OF DAILY DISTANCES TRAVELED 1851[a]

July				August				September			
Day	Miles	Day	Miles	Day	Miles	Day	Miles	Day	Miles	Day	Miles
1	12	17	15	1	15	17	0	1	18	16	16
2	15	18	15	2	20	18	11	2	15	17	13
3	12	19	18	3	0	19	18	3	12	18	20
4	12	20	12	4	20	20	13	4	16	19	5
5	17	21	16	5	27	21	16	5	18	20	15
6	10	22	12	6	3	22	18	6	10	21	14
7	15	23	8	7	22	23	0	7	0	22	13
8	15	24	18	8	20	24	0	8	16	23	14
9	7	25	2	9	18	25	27	9	10	24	7
10	15	26	15	10	11	26	20	10	15	25	16
11	10	27	12	11	15	27	16	11	7	26	14
12	15	28	20	12	19	28	12	12	14	27	12
13	0	29	10	13	14	29	16	13	13	28	15
14	8	30	0	14	20	30	12	14	9	29	16
15	20	31	12	15	18	31	17	15	9	30	5
16	10			16	16			October		1	11

Total miles 1239 [sic]

[a]J. D. T. McAllister Journal (MS, Utah State Historical Society), October 1851, p. 43.

after they were conditioned, stated that his readers might "be surprised at this, and especially when I say that Lizzie walked almost the entire way."[20] The spirit of the "gathering" seemed to make the walking easy. "The truth is you somehow get the spirit of walking, and traveling is not half so bad as it is to sit and think of it."[21] Table 2 indicates the daily mileage and shows the gradual increase in distance traveled as the emigrants became conditioned. With the passage of time, the trail became better and the daily journeys longer. By 1862, some companies were able to make the trip in only two months.[22]

Walking was a part of the daily routine, and emigrants universally commented on it in diaries and letters. Other aspects of the trip received unequal comment. Those aspects of the trip that affected the travelers most received greatest coverage, as would be expected. When people live and travel for extended periods of time without adequate protection from the elements of the environment, the daily weather is of critical interest. Rain, heat, cold, or wind all affected them immediately by rendering more difficult their daily routine of traveling. As would be expected, reports on the daily weather conditions are found in all of the journals.

When the daily weather presented nothing untoward, the following was a normal entry: "The weather is pleasant while it frosted a little at night."[23] When the nights were cold enough to cause discomfort, the emigrants included more information. One diarist compared the cold nights to the fall of the year.[24] The cool nights in the mountains surprised the emigrants and prompted comment: "On these high mountains the nights were, even in the heat of summer, very cold, and water left exposed at night was in the morning found a solid lump of ice."[25]

The warmth encountered in the long days of traveling was commented upon less than the cold. This is undoubtedly because the emigrants, traveling in summer, expected it to be warm, while the coolness was unexpected and hence more noteworthy. With one exception, references to the heat of the day are confined to statements such as "warm day," or to records of the temperature. The exception is the description given by an English woman writing an account of her journey for publication in an English newpaper: "The days were as warm as the nights were cold, and we had to travel with as little covering as

8

possible. Some of us kept our umbrellas up, but we soon found that the strength of the sun burned them to tinder."[26]

Occasions on which it rained received extensive comment from the emigrants. The discomfort caused by rain-soaked clothing, bedding, and fuel was not easily alleviated. Each rainstorm was noted, and the extent of the journal entries reflect the severity of the storm. A typical reaction to a thunderstorm was that "it rained all night, with thunder and lightning the wind blew a perfect hurricane."[27] More severe storms had an even greater impact, causing the emigrants to break up their camps. One diarist records that "in the afternoon a storm arose emitting very violent wind, thunder, lightning, rain and hail. Many tents blew over."[28]

Experiences with rainstorms, with their accompanying discomforts, were primarily limited to the eastern part of the journey. Winds, with dust clouds, however, were encountered throughout the trip. In the grassy prairies near the start of the journey, the winds prompted comment primarily because of their desiccating nature. William Clayton noted that "the wagons and everything else is shrinking up, for the wind is perfectly dry and parching; there is no moisture in it. Even my writing desk is splitting with the drought."[29] Even with the grassy prairies surrounding them, the wind stirred up the dust of the trail. The following day, Clayton remarked that the wind was "blowing from the north tremendously strong, and clouds of dust arose from under the wagon wheels."[30] The trail became ever wider as the Mormon migration increased. Within a few years, dust was a constant companion of the travelers, and any wind made it almost unbearable. Three years after the passage of the first pioneer company, an emigrant on a windy day reported "the road very dusty, a cold high wind makes it very unpleasant traveling."[31]

Another diarist reported "a good days travel of 17 miles but most unpleasant on account of a strong head wind and the dust flying thicker than ever before."[32] It is evident that the wind was important only because of the dust and other discomforts which accompanied it. No diarist reported that the wind depressed them or otherwise affected anything but their physical comfort. The impact of the wind and its accompanying dust was summed up by one diarist who stated with disgust that "it has blown dust enough to choke us all to death."[33]

In all of their comments concerning the weather, it was the unfavorable aspects upon which the emigrants dwelt longest. When the daily weather was neither unusual nor a source of discomfort, comments were restricted to "pleasant" or "very fine." The normal drew little comment; the exceptional a great deal.

Vegetation

Grass

Vegetation or its absence drew almost daily comment by diarists. The travelers were most concerned about grass. The first group of pioneers in 1847, leaving very early in the spring, were faced with the problem of Indians burning the previous year's grass while the northward-migrating buffalo were grazing off and trampling down all the new grass. On May 3, 1847, for example, "the Indians had set fire to the old grass which was among the new and all was burned together."[34] After traveling over the burnt prairie for several days, one emigrant stated: "The prairie is all burned bare and the black ashes fly bad, making the brethren look more like Indians than white folks."[35]

The impact of the buffalo on the grass was also noted. "In many places the grass is fed down by the Buffelows so that it has the appearance of an olde pasture onley the fence is missing."[36] A week and some sixty-four miles later,[37] they reported that the buffalo were still keeping the grass grazed off. Clayton reports that "the prairie is here bare as a poor English pasture, the grass being eaten off by uncountable herds of buffalo."[38] To another emigrant it seemed they were crossing an "immense buffalo pasture" and that "the whole face of the earth is eat up here by the thousands upon thousands of buffalo."[39]

Subsequent emigrant companies left later in the spring and had no buffalo and fires to contend with, but they still commented on the dearth of grass. "We have traveled this forenoon nine miles over barren, sandy land being no grass."[40] The difference between the amount of grass they found and what they thought they would find also drew comment. At the crossing of the Green River, for example, they reported that "the grass grows good and plentiful but not so much as has been represented."[41]

On occasion an emigrant was sufficiently impressed by the grass to take time to describe it. One said of buffalo grass: "It resembles blue

10

grass it is fine and for common not more than from 4 to 6 inches high."[42] While in the prairies of eastern Nebraska, another exclaimed that "there is nothing to see but one boundless sea of grass, waving like the waves of the sea, and now and then a tree."[43] But these grasslands evoked a more favorable response from most travelers, of whom Norton Jacob may be considered representative: "This is a most delightful country of undulating prairie and the slopes crowned with the richest kind of grass."[44]

Trees

Since most of the emigrants came from lands where woods and forests were common, the experience of traveling on the treeless prairies was a novel one. The appearance of any timber was dutifully noted. The pioneer company reported of the landscape west of Omaha, Nebraska, that the river bottoms were very broad, but "destitute of timber."[45] They "had come up the Platt and Loup fork about 130 miles through as fine a contrey as I ever saw for farming or grazing. The great difficulty was the lack of timber."[46] Near present-day Ogallala the soil was rich, but there was "no timber."[47] The appearance of some trees near Scotts Bluff had become noteworthy: "Today we could see a fue trees on the outher side of the River which was a new thing to us for we had not seen such a sight for a long time."[48]

After passing Fort Laramie and entering the mountains then called "The Black Hills," the pioneers remarked on the covering of pine forests whose dark green color, when viewed from a distance, gave the hills their name.[49] The Sweetwater River area had "no timber but dwarf willows throughout its entire length,"[50] and the surrounding country was "entirely destitute of timber, not a tree to be seen, nor a shrub larger than the wild sage."[51] At the Green River crossing, they found cottonwood trees growing, but none "large enough to make a canoe."[52]

Other types of vegetation caught the attention of some emigrants. Clayton typifies this group. He reported on every type of plant they passed, while other emigrants did not mention them unless they were quite obvious. At Ash Hollow, a landmark on the trail, one emigrant remarked on a change in the prairie:

We passed Ash Hollow last Wednesday which presented quite a change of scen-

ery, ... the shrubbery presenting the greatest variety imaginable on wild soil. Several kinds of flowers as delicate and interesting looking as if they were raised in well cultivated gardens of the East ... also appeared.[53]

In the same vicinity, Clayton remarked that he had "noticed a great variety of shrubs, plants and flowers all new" to him.[54]

Other diarists commented on useful plants, or upon flowers whose attractive colors presented a pleasant view. Remarking on the contrast between snowdrifts in the sheltered ravines and the flowers on the exposed slopes, one emigrant pointed out the beauty of the "dandelians in full bloom Strawburys and Goosbrys also were in bloom near by."[55] The wild flax growing along Black's Fork River was also viewed favorably because it was "in sufficient quantity that one could make a hand [of] gathering it."[56]

Climate

From their observations upon weather and vegetation, the emigrants arrived at conclusions regarding the climate in various localities along the trail. From the decreasing height of grass in western Nebraska, they surmised that the "country here is evidently getting drier."[57] Near present-day Evanston, Wyoming, they remarked that the "country evidently lacks rain, even the grass appears parched."[58] The snow on the mountains was viewed as the cause of a "cold" climate.[59] The sagebrush plains of Wyoming were viewed as a sign of "barren" and "sterile" land. "We could look 'til eyes were tired & scarce any end to the dreary wasted of the everlasting Sage Plains."[60] At South Pass another emigrant remarked that they "traveled 24¼ miles over a level but barren country."[61] The monotony of the sage plains was described as: "The most barren, desolate country, nothing to relieve the eye."[62].

The barren nature of the sage plains did not cause the majority of the emigrants to view them as a desert, however. Of 135 diaries examined, only seven contain the word *desert* in referring to any part of the journey (see Table 3). Of these seven, four use the term *desert* to refer only to a particular day's journey.

A typical entry states that they "traveled a bout 15 and a half miles and a bout 6 miles was over a Dessert place."[63] In this context, the authors are speaking of places where even the sage did not grow due to alkali or extremely sandy soil or other localized conditions. The same

TABLE 3

**YEARS IN WHICH THE TERM "DESERT"
APPEARED IN DIARIES**

Year	References to Desert	Male	Female
1847	3	3	0
1848	1	1	0
1850	1	0	1
1851	1	0	1
1861	1	1	0
Totals	7	5	2

diarist reported a few days later that "the country is in Different places Dersert and barren except what they call Devils toungs [cactus] which grows on a Dersert."[64] Any place without either grass or sage growing on it is a desert according to this diarist. On another occasion, he stated that they traveled "over a Dersert 4 miles and came to where there were grass."[65]

Even in the prairies of eastern Nebraska, places which had little grass were viewed as desert places. "Before we reached the Platte bottoms the ground became so saney [sandy] that it looked like a barren desert."[66] One diarist reacted strongly to a particularly trying day's journey: "We roll over a bad road in a desolate country that would remind any-one of the Deserts in Arabia (we read about)."[67]

Viewing this segment of the journey in retrospect, one diarist compared the welcome sight of trees along the Green River to the "long stretch of desert country, through which we have been travelling for the last four weeks."[68] She also viewed the sage plains as a desert while they were journeying through them. "We are among the Rocky mountains. The country is a desert except here and there a patch of grass by the side of the small streams."[69]

The Mormons were either unfamiliar with the term *Great American Desert* or failed to apply it to the country they traveled, for no diarists used the term in connection with their journey.[70]

The vast majority of the Mormons were utilitarian in their view of the sage plains, and all elements of the environment. Grass was sufficient for their oxen, water was available several times each day, at least, and the land was essentially covered by sufficient vegetation that it did not warrant the name *desert*. Only in describing scenic views did the Mormons allow themselves poetic license, and even then they tended to be restrained.

Realistic appraisal is never more evident than in their assessments of the suitability for settlement and agriculture of the lands they passed on their journey. The section of the journey from Winter Quarters to Fort Laramie was replete wih suitable settlement sites. The first 100 miles of their journey was through "as fine a contrey as ever I saw for farming or grazing," wrote Jackman.[71] Of the same region Clayton noted that the "soil looks black and no doubt would yield a good crop of corn."[72]

By contrast there were some places too poor for agriculture. "I have no idea that corn would grow here for the land is very dry and loose and sandy and appears poor," remarked Clayton of one location.[73] Such infertile sites were outnumbered, however, by the many choice agricultural sites found in the prairies of Nebraska. Along the Loup Fork River, the land was level and "beautiful for a farm."[74] The suitability of the land for settlement was summed up by one emigrant who pointed out that those who viewed the prairies of eastern Nebraska as sterile and forbidding were misinformed:

This is a most delightful country of undulating prairie and the slopes crowned with the richest kind of grass. . . . This country is so beautifully adapted to cultivation that there is driven from the mind all idea of its being a wild waste in the wilderness. The fields in the woods and the habitations of men one is continually looking out for.[75]

The eminently suitable land in eastern Nebraska was in sharp contrast to that found in the portion of the trip through Wyoming. There, most of the land was unsuited to the type of agriculture the Mormons had experienced. Most of it was characterized as "sterile" and "barren." However, small valleys which offered an opportunity for agricul-

14

ture did receive favorable comment: "The land here on the bottom is rich and would doubtless yield good crops of grain and potatoes, etc."[76]

It is of interest that the appraisal of the various lands with regard to their agricultural potential was restricted to the pioneer company of 1847. Subsequent emigrants, aware that the Church did not intend to settle those regions through which they passed, paid little attention to their suitablity for settlement. Many of the travelers, however, responded to the landmarks and curiosities along the trail, as Table 4 indicates. While many diaries are so terse that references to any natural features are excluded, the comments of the more articulate diarists point out that all the emigrants visited the important landmarks.[77]

Landmarks

At an early date, certain landscape features became landmarks to the Mormon pioneers. These were formalized partially by William Clayton in a Mormon guidebook which the emigrants studied,[78] and partially by other travelers to Oregon and California. These landmarks became both mileposts by which progress on the journey was measured, and curiosities that the emigrants visited. Visits to these landmarks helped alleviate the monotony of the daily journeying, and the desire to visit them was such that even after traveling all day, they were willing to walk farther to visit them. "After we camped by the Sweet Water [River] I took a tramp of 1½ miles to see the Devil's gate which we passed but could not see to advantage at that time," noted the articulate Martha Heywood.[79]

Geological Formations

The early part of the trip lacked conspicuous landscape elements. But when the pioneers arrived at Ash Hollow, they entered an area noted for high, scenic bluffs along the North Platte River. Some particular isolated geological formations received special attention because they had distinctive appearances or had acquired names. The first encountered was Courthouse Rock, then Chimney Rock, Scotts Bluff, and Independence Rock.

At one point, the Sweetwater River formed a chasm through which it rushed swiftly. This chasm, known as Devil's Gate, was another

TABLE 4

RESPONSES TO LANDMARKS ON THE MORMON TRAIL

Number of diaries by year	Landmark											
	Bluff Ruins	Courthouse Rock	Chimney Rock	Scotts Bluff	Fort Laramie	Independence Rock	Devil's Gate	First view of mountains	South Pass	Wasatch Mountains	Scenic views and panoramas	Curiosities
1847 (22)[a]	17	8	15	12	18	17	15	18	14	16	17	18
1848 (13)	5	3	6	3	7	5	6	6	5	3	5	6
1849 (6)	3	2	3	1	3	3	3	3	3	2	3	2
1850 (6)	4	4	4	3	4	3	3	2	3	4	4	4
1851 (9)	3	2	3	1	3	3	3	3	3	3	2	2
1852 (14)	6	1	3	5	7	5	5	6	4	4	4	5
1853 (7)	3	0	3	2	4	4	3	3	3	2	3	3
1854 (6)	4	2	4	3	3	3	2	4	3	3	3	4
1855 (5)	2	1	3	1	3	3	2	2	2	2	3	2
1856 (7)	3	2	3	2	4	3	3	4	2	2	3	3
1857 (8)	4	3	4	3	5	5	5	4	4	4	5	4
1858 (5)	3	1	3	2	3	3	2	3	2	2	3	3
1859 (4)	1	1	3	2	3	3	2	3	2	3	3	2
1860 (7)	4	2	3	2	4	4	3	4	3	2	4	4
1861 (5)	2	1	2	1	2	1	2	1	1	1	1	2
1862 (2)	1	0	1	1	1	1	1	1	1	1	1	1
1863 (2)	0	0	1	0	1	1	2	1	2	2	2	2
1864 (0)	0	0	0	0	0	0	0	0	0	0	0	0
1865 (4)	2	2	3	2	3	3	2	4	3	2	4	4
1866 (3)	2	2	2	2	3	3	2	2	2	1	3	3
Total 135	69	37	69	48	81	73	65	74	62	59	73	74

[a]Each number in parentheses indicates the total number of diaries examined for the year. Many (56) of the diaries made no comment about anything but events within the camp, or only made a few random entries concerning the trip.

16

landmark on the journey. As with the other landmarks, the Mormons felt compelled to visit it. To the emigrants, "it was a curiosity."[80]

Fort Laramie

Fort Laramie was a landmark since it was the first contact with a settlement since the departure of the emigrants from Winter Quarters. Aside from its importance as a supply center and diversion from the trail, Fort Laramie was important because near it the mountains first appeared on the horizon.

The Rocky Mountains

The first view of the mountains was an emotional event; in addition to their stark grandeur, the Rockies heralded the change from the plains segment to the mountain segment of the journey. The first appearance of the mountains was also an indication that the Mormons were nearing their new home. The diarists noted their first view of the mountains, and the following is a representative reaction to this first view: "I have seen the Rocky mountains for the first time today. They look stupendous in the dim opaque of the horizon and but a faint line marking their existence and altitude. The highest one is called 'Laramie peak.' "[81]

Travelers commented about the snow on the mountains because it was something they had not seen previously during the summer months. A typical entry states that the mountains covered with snow "look a little odd at this season of the year."[82] As the emigrants traveled farther west and came closer to the mountains, they described them in poetic fashion:

The wind river chain of the rocky mountains which was discovered yesterday, but the shaded side towards us, shone dimly, but now stands forth in all the noon day brilliancy of a summer's sun and robed in full winter costume, presents a scene majestic grand and imposing. the eternal snows lifted up on those angular peaks towards heaven an offering from earth to heaven's King: as though she would fain enjoy his purity.[83]

Others were overwhelmed by the sheer size of the mountains, and their views reflect the mental dichotomy between being exhilarated by the beauty and being humbled by the massiveness.[84]

South Pass

South pass was one of the most important landmarks on the overland journey. It marked the division between the Atlantic drainage and that of the Pacific. As such, it was viewed by the Mormons as the beginning of the descent which would culminate in their new home in the Great Basin. While the diarists remarked upon their arrival at South Pass, thcy only noted that it was very unprepossessing because of its gentle slope and great width. "You will not know when you are in the South Pass, until all of a sudden you find the water running in an opposite direction—that is towards the west," commented Thomas Bullock.[85]

The Canyons and Mountains of Utah

From South Pass the emigrants traveled through a series of mountains and valleys, the most rugged of which was the Wasatch Range. The scenery here received great praise. Coupled with favorable views of the scenery, however, were remarks about the "narrow" canyons and "terrible roads." The following view contains both praise for the scenic beauty and disgust at the condition of the trail:

Of all the splendid scenery and awful roads that have ever been since creation, I think this day's journey has beaten them all. . . . The road . . . was completely covered with stones as large as bushel boxes, stumps of trees, with here and there mudholes in which our oxen sunk to the knees. Added to this was Kanyon Creek a stream of water running at the bottom of a deep ravine, which interceded our road in such a zigzag fashion, that we had to ford it 16 times, at a descent of 15 to 20 feet and of course as equal ascent [from the crossing].[86]

The magnificence of the scenery made up, at least in part, for the trials of the road:

The grandeur of the scenery to my mind takes away all fear, and while standing in admiration at the view of Milton's expressions in this "Paradise Lost," came forcibly to my recollection. "These are thy glorious works. Parents of good, in wisdom hast thou made them all," and I seemed to forget all the hardships.[87]

Others commented on the "romantic" scenery provided by the combination of high mountains and narrow canyons.[88] The tortuous nature of the last miles of the journey helped to create in the emigrants a

18

heightened sense of anticipation of the welcome end to traveling, and this favorably affected their initial impressions of their new home in the Salt Lake Valley. The scenic panorama which met their gaze when they finally emerged from the Wasatch Mountains, while only one of many scenic views the emigrants had observed, was the most important because it signaled the end of their journey—it was the Zion they had long anticipated.

Scenic Views on the Trip across
the Plains

The most significant factor of the Mormon experience in crossing the plains is that all of the emigrants who made statements about the physical environment along the route reacted favorably to the sights they viewed. Scarcely a day passed without the emigrants' finding something that was "magnificent," "sublime," or "beautiful." This reflects the manner in which they approached the trip. To the travelers, it was a new and unique experience, and each new scenic view called forth effusive praise. Such a reaction is understandable, since any break in the monotony of the dust and fatigue of the day's travel which did not cause more discomfort would certainly be a welcome occurrence. The discomforts of the mode of travel of the Mormon emigrants provided them with a contrast which made scenic views even more attractive.

Panoramic Views

Statements by the more reticent travelers were confined to reports of "beautiful scenery on both sides."[89] Others became more ecstatic over the panoramas that unfolded before them. Commenting on the scenery along the Platte River, one emigrant stated that "here we saw some of the finest scenery we have seen on our journey. The Platt winding at our feet the sun shining on it causing it to look like a ribbon of silver surrounding hills and masses of rocks in all shapes like ancient ruins form quite an interesting picture."[90]

Statements about the "romantic" nature of the scenery were common. At the Loup Fork River crossing, one diarist stated: "There is something romantic in the scenery around here, and the prospect cannot well be exaggerated."[91] Other scenes evoked comparisons with the former homes of the emigrants. "This place reminds me of England.

The calm, still morning with the warbling of many birds, the rich grass, good streams, and plenty of timber, make it pleasant."[92]

Sunsets provided magnificent views to the travelers. The opportunity to rest from their travels made them appear even more beautiful. The Platte appeared as "a line of silver glistening in the setting sun through the scattered timber."[93] The varied features created among the clouds by the setting sun were most spectacular: "When the sun was setting the sky presented the most Noble Grand & glorious appearance we ever beheld. at one time it appeared as if there were splendid Palaces Castles and Land Scenery."[94]

The mountains offered views that were "wild and picturesque."[95] "Very romantic scenery all day. . . . The country for the last three days has been beyond description for wilderness and beauty."[96] All of the diarists responded positively both to the views of the mountains and the clarity of the atmosphere in the high altitudes. The emigrants also remarked on the difficulties of judging distances accurately both in the mountain country and in the plains. "The air is so clear that Objects a mile off only appear to be a few yards."[97] The difficulty of judging distance was especially noted by those who were assigned to act as hunters for the emigrant parties. "Objects are seen at double the distance that they can be in the Mississippi Valley. We are very liable to be deceived as to distances."[98] The distance misconception was noted because it was a new experience, as were many sights along the trail.

Curiosities

Anything out of the ordinary was of interest to the emigrants, and because it provided a distraction from the trail it was viewed favorably. Some idea of the interest with which these curiosities were approached is indicated by the following wry statement by William Clayton after tasting the water of a mineral spring: "After traveling three and a half miles we passed a small copperas spring at the foot of a mountain a little to the left of the road. The water is very clear but tastes very strong of copperas and alum and has a somewhat singular effect on the mouth."[99] Other curiosities included "saleratus ponds" where they gathered "saleratus" to use in making bread,[100] an ice spring where good-tasting ice was found under sulphur-impregnated water, the first experience with alkali-covered land, and a tar spring.

Even an invasion of grasshoppers offered a "wonderful sight": "About 7 we had another heavy swarm of grasshoppers at this time everything is covered and millions in the air we never saw such a wonderful sight before."[101] As previously indicated, the Saints found any diversion welcome if it did not contribute to the unpleasant aspects of the journeying. Thus even the grasshoppers—which later became a scourge to those who settled these lands—were viewed favorably.

Conclusion

The accounts of the Mormon migrants who made the overland journey to Utah are much different from the later descriptions of the journey. With the exception of the handcart companies, the Mormon travelers reported only the discomfort and inconvenience caused by rain or dust. The journey itself was described in positive terms, with each new scenic panorama, each famous landmark, and each unusual feature along the trail described favorably. The emigrants did not say that the environment through which they passed was a "desert," although occasional stretches of the trail without grass were viewed as desertlike. So long as there was vegetation covering the soil, and water for drinking at reasonable intervals, the land was described as "prairies" or "plains."

The journey itself was described as an enjoyable experience, one which gained symbolic importance in providing the converts, with their divergent backgrounds, a common experience. All were forced to meet the challenge of the tedious days of travel, and the experience gained in the communal effort aided them in their transition from the individualistic societies they had left to the cooperative system of the Mormon village. Additionally, it allowed an assessment of the character of the migrants. "I can assure you that 'Mormon' traveling is to a great extent good, in letting you see people in their true colours," noted one migrant.[102] As an event, the overland journey marked a hiatus in the normal day-to-day activities of making a livelihood. For most of the migrants, the journey was a one-way, one-time event. On the whole, the accounts of those who recorded their experiences points out that the overland journey was more a "pleasuring excursion" than a trip through a "howling, trackless desert."

The important question is why the enjoyment and the favorable reactions of the typical Mormon migrant to the overland journey are not reflected in the official accounts, which detail the great difficulty of crossing a "desert" area. The primary causes seem to involve the normal tendency to magnify events as they are recollected later, combined with rhetoric of leaders describing an event which was manifestly deserving of accolade. The Mormon achievement in moving some 60,000 souls across the plains in the two decades from 1847 to the coming of the railroad in 1869 is of heroic magnitude. When described later, the importance of the symbolic nature of the overland trip led to the magnification of its difficulty. The orations of July 24 celebrations would be rather mundane if they emphasized the relative ease of the overland journey.

The tendency for hyperbole to surround a heroic event when it is publicly recounted was accented by the disaster which did strike some of the handcart companies. The difficulties of the Martin and Willie companies of the handcart pioneers seem to have been adopted as the norm rather than the exception. The tragedy of the handcart pioneers overshadows the journey of the other tens of thousands of Mormon migrants. But the achievement of those thousands of migrants who did not die, who walked over a thousand miles through dust, rain, cold, and sun, is no less heroic. For the converts from field and factory to undertake such a journey, bringing wives, children, aged, and infirm along, is a miracle of itself. It would be unfortunate if the hyperbole hid the fact that these were ordinary men, women, and children; for it is their humanness which made the overland journey miraculous. Their accomplishment was epic enough: it need not be embroidered with raging deserts.

Notes

1. Sermon by George A. Smith, in *Journal of Discourses*, 26 vols. (London: Latter-day Saints' Book Depot, 1855–86), 9(1861):66.

2. Sermon by Erastus Snow, ibid., 16(1873):206.

3. Letter from Thomas Bullock to the Saints in England, *Millennial Star*, 14(1852):300 (hereinafter cited as *MS*).

4. Sermon by George A. Smith, ibid., 2(1855):329.

5. Sermon by George A. Smith, in *Journal of Discourses*, 9(1861):73.

6. Letter from _________ to his brother and sister dated Great Salt Lake City, October 28, 1854, in *MS*, 17(1855):172.

7. Formerly Winter Quarters.

8. Mary Senior to her parents, October 6, 1862, in *MS* 24(1862)781:82.

9. Reprinted from *New York Tribune*, n.p., n.d., in *MS* 17(1855):42.

10. Joseph Smith, *The Doctrine and Covenants of the Church of Jesus Christ of Latter-day Saints* (Salt Lake City: George Q. Cannon and Sons, 1891), p. 489.

11. Norton Jacob Diary, January 14, 1847, pp. 47– 48, Utah State Historical Society, Salt Lake City.

12. William Clayton, *William Clayton's Journal* (Salt lake City: Clayton Family Association, 1921), February 18, 1847, pp. 80–81. The ruling on having guns cocked was dropped after one of Brigham Young's horses was accidentally shot when a gun discharged after the hammer caught on something as it was being pulled out of the back of a wagon.

13. Ibid., April 16, 1847, p. 51. Instruction by Heber C. Kimball.

14. *MS* 25(1863):59–60.

15. William Fuller to his wife's parents in Basingstoke, England, recounting journey of 1862, ibid., 25(1863):61.

16. Report on the journey of the 1847 pioneers by Thomas Bullock, ibid., 10(1848):61.

17. A correspondent listed as Mary Senior, reporting on her trip of 1861, ibid., 24(1862):781.

18. Report on the journey of A. N. MacFarlane in 1868, reprinted from *Dundee Advertiser*, n.d., n.p., ibid., 30(1868):818.

19. Ibid. This cheerfulness is important in understanding the Mormons' perception of their journey. Taught to look at the positive side of things, and having a high degree of order that eliminated most of the hardships faced by other immigrants, the Mormons were able to respond favorably to most aspects of the environment.

20. William Fuller to wife's parents in Basingstoke, England, ibid., 25(1863):60.

21. The idea that walking was not difficult was apparently held by other emigrants, since of ninety-seven letters appearing in the *Millennial Star* between 1848 and 1868 describing the journey, twenty-one commented on the relative ease of walking, and none indicated that it was a hardship.

22. See *MS* 24(1862):781.

23. Jacob Diary, April 7, 1847, just west of Council Bluffs, Iowa.

24. William A. Empey Journal, August 1, 1847, Utah State Historical Society.

25. *MS* 30(1868):819.

26. Report on the journey of A. N. MacFarlane in 1868, reprinted from *Dundee Advertizer*, n.p., n.d., in ibid., 30(1868):819.

27. Mary Ann Maughan Journal, July 1, 1850, Utah State Historical Society. Just west of present-day Kearney, Nebraska.

28. Clayton, *William Clayton's Journal*, May 6, 1846, p. 29.

29. Ibid., April 29, 1847, pp. 112–13.

30. Ibid., April 30, 1847, p. 115.

31. Maughan Journal, August 11, 1850.

32. Martha Heywood Diary (MS, Utah State Historical Society), September 24, 1850.

33. Mary Elizabeth Lightner Journal (MS, Utah State Historical Society), May 3, 1847, p. 79.

34. Levi Jackman Journal, May 3, 1847, p. 79, Utah State Historical Society.

35. Clayton, *William Clayton's Journal*, May 5, 1847, p. 132.

36. Jackman Journal, May 2, 1847, p. 78.

37. Andrew Jenson, "Day by Day with the Utah pioneers, 1847" (MS, Brigham Young University Library), p. 1, gives distance traveled each day.

38. Clayton, *William Clayton's Journal*, May 8, 1847, p. 137. Clayton reported on May 6 that "some think we have passed fifty, and some even a hundred thousand [buffalo] during the day."

39. Jacob Diary, May 3, 1847, p. 71, and May 8, 1847, p. 71.

40. Clayton, *William Clayton's Journal*, June 20, 1847, p. 249.

41. Ibid., June 30, 1847, p. 281.

42. Jackman Journal, May 2, 1847. Near present-day Kearney, Nebraska.

43. Sophia Hardy Journal, June 29, 1850, p. 2., Utah State Historical Society

44. Jacob Diary, April 22, 1847, pp. 55–56. Near present-day Columbus, Nebraska.

45. Ibid., April 19, 1847, p. 54.

46. Jackman Journal, April 23, 1847. At the site of the old Pawnee fort where pioneers crossed Loup Fork River.

47. Clayton, *William Clayton's Journal*, May 15, 1847, p. 151.

48. Jackman Journal, May 28, 1847, p. 88.

49. Clayton, *William Clayton's Journal*, June 7, 1847, p. 221.

50. Jacob Diary, June 26, 1847, p. 103.

51. Clayton, *William Clayton's Journal*, June 20, 1847, p. 250.

52. Ibid., June 30, 1847, pp. 280–81.

53. Heywood Diary, August 15, 1850, p. 8. West of present-day Ogallala, Nebraska.

54. Clayton, *William Clayton's Journal*, May 22, 1847, p. 175.

55. Jackman Journal, June 26, 1847, p. 100.

56. Jacob, Diary, July 7, 1847, p. 108.

57. Ibid., May 22, 1847, p. 80.

58. Clayton, *William Clayton's Journal*, July 12, 1847, p. 292.

59. Jacob Diary, June 29, 1847, p. 105; and Clayton, *William Clayton's Journal*, June 25, 1847, p. 275.

60. John Pulsipher Journal, August 1, 1848, p. 42, Brigham Young University Library.

61. John R. Shinn Journal, July 23, 1850, p. 15, Brigham Young University Library.

62. Lightner Journal, July 27, 1863, p. 36. West of Fort Laramie.

63. Empey Journal, May 22, 1847, p. 5. Near Chimney Rock.

64. Ibid., May 28, 1847, p. 6. Near the present-day Nebraska-Wyoming border. Orson Pratt describes these "Devil toungs," which he says grow "on top of some of these sand hills, in the driest places."

65. Ibid., May 30, 1847, p. 7.

66. Jackman Journal, April 27, 1847, p. 76. Crossing sand hills between Loup Fork River and Platte River.

67. Sixtus E. Johnson Journal, September 16, 1861, p. 33, Brigham Young University Library. Near present-day Green River, Wyoming.

68. Jean Rio Pearce Journal, September 15, 1851, p. 51, Brigham Young University Library.

69. Ibid., August 29, 1851, p. 47.

70. The only reference to the Great American Desert was to the land between the Humboldt and Carson rivers in Nevada, rather than to the western Great Plains region: "We broke camp at 2 p.m. and started on to the Great American Desert." William Henry Branch Journal, June 18, 1856, p. 29, Brigham Young University Library. He emigrated to Utah in 1850.

71, Jackman Journal, April 23, 1847, p. 72.

72. Clayton, *William Clayton's Journal*, April 22, 1847, p. 90.

73. Ibid., April 21, 1847, p. 88.

74. Ibid., April 23, 1847, pp. 93–94.

75. Jacob Diary, April 22, 1847, pp. 55–56.

76. Clayton, *William Clayton's Journal*, June 10, 1847, p. 230. Near present-day Glenrock, Wyoming.

77. Heywood Diary, September 8, 1850, p. 17. The diarist notes under this date that every member of the company but two climbed Independence Rock, and those two were too sick to leave their beds in the wagons.

78. William Clayton, *The Latter-day Saints' Emigrant's Guide: Being a Table of Distances...* (St. Louis: Republican Steam Power Press, Chambers and Knapp, 1848).

79. Heywood Diary, September 8, 1850, p. 17.

80. Ibid.

81. Heywood Diary, August 25, 1850, p. 12.

82. Jackman Journal, June 27, 1847, p. 101.

83. Jacob Diary, June 24, 1847, p. 101.

84. Pearce Journal, August 29, 1851, p. 47.

85. Letter from Thomas Bullock, who accompanied the pioneer company in 1847, *MS* 10(1848):117.

86. Pearce Journal, September 28, 1851, p. 55.

87. Ibid.

88. Clayton, *William Clayton's Journal*, July 16, 1847, p. 296.

89. James Farmer Diary, August 11, 1853, p. 23, Utah State Historical Society.

90. Johnson Journal, August 14, 1861, p. 11.

91. Clayton, *William Clayton's Journal*, April 23, 1847, p. 94.

92. Ibid., June 11, 1847, p. 230. Near Casper, Wyoming.

93. Jacob Diary, April 16, 1847, p. 50. About twenty miles west of Omaha.

94. Elijah Larkin Journal, September 6, 1863, p. 487, Brigham Young University Library.

95. Hardy Journal, October 3, 1850, p. 15.

96. Pearce Journal, September 21, 1851, p. 53.

97. Larkin Journal, September 14, 1863, p. 492.

98. Jacob Diary, May 21, 1847, p. 79.

99. Clayton, *William Clayton's Journal,* July 10, 1847, p. 287.

100. Jackman Journal, June 21, 1847, p. 97.

101. Farmer Diary, August 19, 1853, p. 27.

102. Letter dated Great Salt Lake City, October 28, 1854, in *MS* 17(1855):172.

Mormon Exploration in the Lower Colorado River Area

Melvin T. Smith

The lower Colorado River region is desert, devoid of water except for infrequent springs and the rivers which pass through it. Its ridges and valleys are lava-strewn, sharply eroded, and sandblown. The flora and fauna are limited. The limited arable lands have long been claimed by the native American residents.

The area is less than one hundred miles square, bounded on the east by the Grand Canyon, on the north by the Virgin and Muddy rivers, on the west by Las Vegas Wash, and on the south by the Needles. The Colorado River flows west across several ranges and valleys before turning south at the Great Bend, approximately where Hoover Dam is now located. From there it pursues its course southward some four hundred miles to the Gulf of California (see Figure 1).

For the Mormons and others, this region generally held interest for several reasons: the potential navigation of the Colorado, the mild climate and irrigable lands, the minerals ranging in value from silver to salt, and its proximity to a year-round route between California and Utah. Mormons looked to this region for a seaport, as a freight and emigrant route, and for missions and settlements as part of their quest for political self-determination, isolation and protection, and economic independence and survival.

The Mormons' interest in the Colorado River had existed as early as 1846,[1] and soon after settlement began in the Salt Lake Valley, the Mormons moved south to freight and to explore.[2] By 1849 the Mormon-California Trail[3] had been established, and the settlement at Provo that same year caused Brigham Young to speculate on "a seaport in California *or* at the head of the Gulf of California" (namely the

29

Mormon Exploration
Along the Colorado
St. George
Muddy
River
Millersberg
Virgin
River
St. Thomas
Las Vegas
Callville
Bonelli's
Ferry
Pearce's Ferry
Vegas Wash
Boulder Canyon
Black
Canyon
Grand
Canyon
Eldorado
Canyon
Cottonwood Island
Kingman
Pyramid
Canyon
Hardyville
Needles
Nv.
Ut.
Ca.
Az.

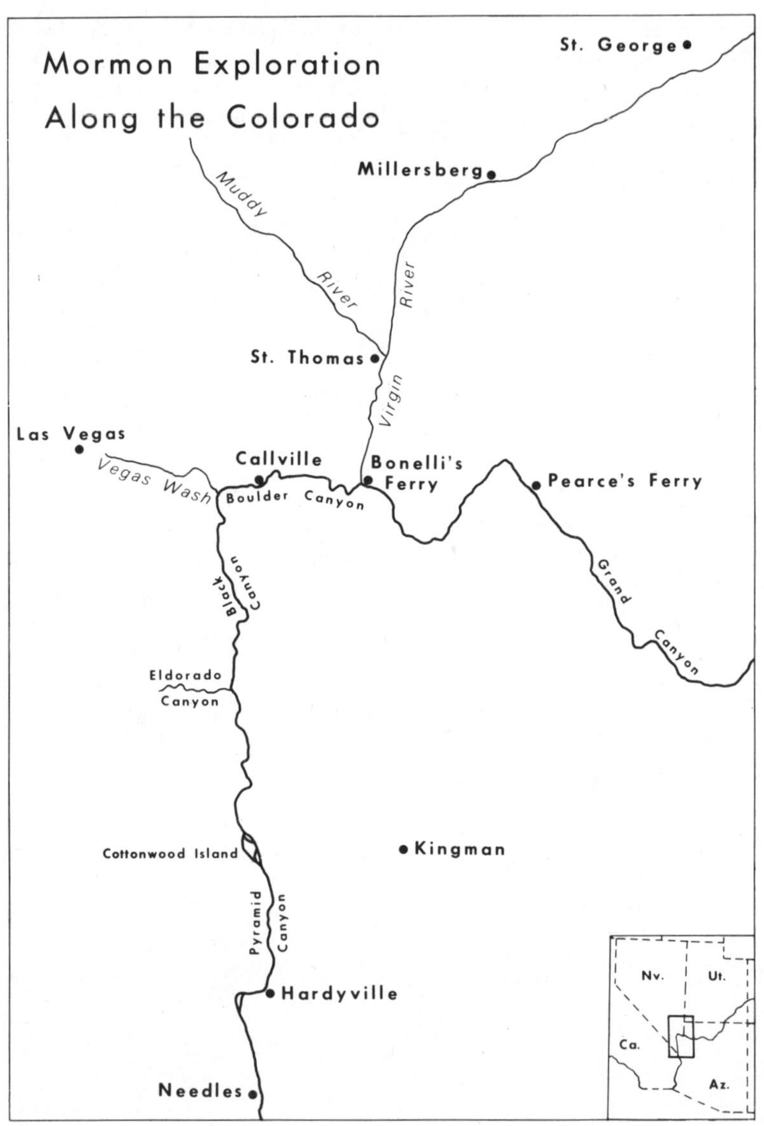

FIGURE 1

Colorado River).[4] Simultaneously, Mormon leaders were seeking to establish their State of Deseret with boundaries allowing such seaports; but Congress in 1850 proved to be much less generous, with the establishment of the territory of Utah.

By 1850, Parley P. Pratt's party had explored to the Virgin River.[5] Parowan was settled within a year and San Bernardino, California, the summer following (1851). Travelers between the two regions passed within twenty-five miles of the Colorado's Great Bend near Las Vegas. That overland trek was tedious, the freighting difficult, and water and forage scarce. It is no surprise that Mormons remained interested in the Colorado River during the next few years.

One of the first United States government surveys on the river was conducted by Lt. George Derby during the winter of 1850–51.[6] Upon hearing of the expedition, Brigham Young wrote to Apostles Rich and Lyman in San Bernardino to "be on the alert" as to the river's navigability and the settlement potential along its banks.[7] President Young also postulated use of the California route for Mormon emigration.[8]

For some reason the expeditions of Major Samuel P. Heintzelman (1850) and of Lt. Lorenzo Sitgreaves (1851) failed to attract Mormon reaction, although Sitgreaves believed the river navigable at least to the Needles, only seventy-five miles below the Great Bend.[9] Perhaps the Mormons were simply too preoccupied with other concerns.

During these years Brigham Young organized the Southern Indian Mission. It was the missionaries to the Indians who first explored the area defined in this paper and who established contacts with the Indians. The Southern Indian Mission also moved the Mormons onto the Virgin River. In 1852 John D. Lee moved south to Fort Harmony. Jacob Hamblin and colleagues were on the Santa Clara by the spring of 1854. These moves were significant to later Mormon involvement with the Colorado River.

In 1853, as a part of the nation's drive for a transcontinental railroad, Lt. A. M. Whipple explored westward along the 35th parallel through northern Arizona. His route crossed the Colorado River above the Needles, where he became very much aware of the Mormon presence in the Southwest,[10] and they of him. The *Deseret News* (May 11, 1854) summarized his report. That fall, Elder D. M. Thomas reported to the *News* that California Senator William H. Gwin was promising to construct a railroad to the Colorado River at Yuma. Thomas further suggested that goods could be shipped to Salt Lake City via the Colorado to the mouth of the Virgin River, "to which navigation is said to be good."[11]

By April conference, 1855, President Young had decided to expand the Southern Indian Mission. William Bringhurst and party were called to establish a post at Vegas Springs. They were to convert the Indians and then baptize them, or vice versa. In addition, they were to explore for land, water, and mineral resources.[12] More particularly, missionaries under Rufus C. Allen, Southern Indian Mission president, were to explore the Colorado River to determine its navigability. Allen and Bringhurst arrived at Las Vegas together in mid-June. The explorers proceeded southeast to the Great Bend, then south fifteen miles along the Colorado's west bank into the rugged lava ridges that formed Black Canyon, before turning back to Las Vegas.

Allen speculated that the river was navigable to that point. Still, he had little specific information to report to Brigham Young.[13] Even so the Las Vegas missionaries continued optimistic. George W. Bean reported in October 1855 that "we will take sail down the Colorado and visit our friends at Fort Umah [sic] or go visit the Indians along the shore."[14] As late as December of that year Governor Young reported favorably on the project to the territorial legislature.[15] Bringhurst began 1856 with another exploration of the river,[16] but learned little. Within a year, the Las Vegas Mission itself was practically defunct.[17] The optimism and initiative of 1855 were frustrated by the harsh realities of the region. Mormon expectations based on rumors and speculation did not put steamboats at their doorsteps, nor Mormon souls into the lowly Lamanites.

Mormon impact on the area's exploration was greater indirectly than it had been through their own expeditions. For example, Lt. Sylvester Mowry traveled from Salt Lake City to Las Vegas in June 1855, where he learned of river exploration plans. Upon reaching Fort Tejon, California, Mowry reported to his superiors on Mormon activity in the area and sought funds for a survey of the river to be conducted by himself.[18] While this request was not granted, Captain T. J. Cram, U.S. Army Department of the Pacific, asked for $10,000 for a survey of the Colorado River, followed by Captain Rufus Ingall's recommendation that the Colorado River be used to freight supplies into Salt

Lake City.[19] In the summer of 1856 the army assigned such a survey to Lt. Joseph C. Ives.

The events of 1857, particularly the coming of Johnston's Army and the Mountain Meadows Massacre, forced a reshuffling of Mormon priorities. Southern Indian missionaries, under the new presidency of Jacob Hamblin, were assigned to protect the wagon trains between Southern Utah and California from further Indian harrassments. They also helped California Saints returning along the route to gather into the mountains.[20]

When rumors of the proposed U.S. government expeditions reached Hamblin, his missionaries then became scouts, spies, and Indian ambassadors. As such they formed new defensive alliances with the Indian tribes in the region. This latter role generated two expeditions along the Colorado River. First, Ira Hatch and Dudley Leavitt ventured as far south as Cottonwood Island in late 1857 and nearly lost their lives at the hands of the hostile Mojave Indians. Hatch and Leavitt gave few details about the river, since their interest had been in the Indians themselves.[21]

In March of 1858, Jacob Hamblin led a party of three men (Sam Knight, Thales Haskell, and Dudley Leavitt) south to the river, where they intercepted Lt. Joseph Ives on his steamer *Explorer*.[22] Hamblin's primary objective was spying, which he accomplished with little success. Lt. Ives discovered the Mormons before they did him, and he clearly saw through Haskell's claims of disaffection from the Mormons. In addition, Hamblin misinterpreted Ives's mission, although Ives proclaimed it clearly, and Hamblin misread Ives's signals and the Indians' rumors to believe that Ive's packtrain was indeed an army coming upriver to invade Zion.[23] Overreaction is not uncommon in wartime, and Hamblin's party was successful in creating suspicion and hostility among the Mojave Indians toward the Ives expedition.

As for Lt. Ives, his party succeeded in reaching lower Black Canyon. They rowed a skiff up to Vegas Wash and declared the Colorado navigable to that point. In spite of mistaking Vegas Wash for the Virgin River, Ives's expedition submitted excellent reports on the river, the land, and the Indians, a tribute to professionals with resources.

The rumors rampant with the Mormon War produced one final expedition in April 1858. Apostle Amasa Lyman believed that a major invasion up the Colorado River was likely. After reporting this intelligence to Brigham Young in February, Lyman rushed south to Cedar City and organized a party of twenty capable men who, with Ira Hatch as guide, reached Las Vegas on April 15, 1858. Lyman's party proceeded south, located a defensive site in Pyramid Canyon (should it be needed), and noted good agriculture lands in the Cottonwood and Mojave valleys. Lyman also confirmed that no invading army was on the river. His expedition, while prompted by a false assumption, was successful and carefully recorded.[24] Yet it was Ives's report, not Lyman's, that was published in the *Deseret News* later that summer.[25] Hamblin recalled his remaining two missionaries from Las Vegas in the spring of 1858;[26] and by June the Mormon War was over. That same season, a cotton experiment farm was operated at Heber (now Bloomington)[27] on the Virgin River. Utah's Dixie had become a fact of Mormon life.

In summary, Mormon explorations into this region during the 1850s were conducted almost exclusively by the Southern Indian missionaries; and with the exception of Rufus Allen's 1855 expedition, exploration was undertaken as a secondary function to the other more pressing issues of secure freight lines, Indian conversions and alliances, defenses for the Saints, and settlements.

The missionaries proved to be brave, dedicated men who knew the Indians. However, careful and competent explorers they were not. Even Amasa Lyman's April 1858 expedition, though superior to the others, in no way approached the standards of the U.S. Army Corps of Engineers. But then Lyman had neither the time nor the resources to field such competence. In each of these situations, Mormons explored in reaction to rumored other forces—prospective navigation of the Colorado River and threats of an invading army. Further, the Las Vegas Mission's hoped-for success in 1855 looked to navigation of the Colorado as an important element in that success. That that prospect was not realized explains in part the mission's short life. By 1860, it was obvious that the Southern Indian Mission was giving way to the Cotton Mission as the primary force focusing Mormon attention on the region under discussion.

As an extension of a policy of economic independence and self-sufficiency, Utah's Dixie offered particular attractions for raising cotton. But there were several major problems. First of all, cotton had to be produced in some quantity to have utility for the Saints. Hence, if the leaders continued a policy of cotton growing, additional people and land in that area would be needed; and that meant expansion west and south along the Virgin River. Secondly, cotton was a cash crop, not a subsistence one, which meant that its utility depended upon other markets either within Zion or without; and markets depended to a great degree upon competitive freight routes, which the region under discussion did not come by naturally. Further, commercial agriculture depended on irrigation from the Virgin River, whose summer rampages not only washed out dams in the river but also filled ditches and laterals with sand. With no irrigation, crops soon withered and died. For the cotton missionaries, no crop often meant no food, since they had to sell cotton to buy what they needed. The struggle would remain in balance for years, often tipping toward the "Undammed Virgin." When settlers finally began to raise lucerne (alfalfa), they had feed to sustain their stock, since this crop could survive a few weeks of drought subsequent to a broken dam. Settlers also ate the young lucerne as greens early in the spring. Its strong physic action was appropriately termed "lucerne hell."[28]

The decade of the 1860s also brought the Civil War. Many Mormons, including leaders, viewed the holocaust as a kind of divine judgment on the wicked.[29] It also seemed to confirm the Mormon need for economic independence. So in October 1861, Brigham Young called several hundred families to be cotton missionaries to Utah's Dixie.[30] However, this injection of people brought only temporary relief. The next three years proved difficult in the extreme.

This paper is particularly concerned with decisions and actions of 1864 and 1865. Changes at the national level continued to have an impact on the Mormons. The Civil War and a series of Indian uprisings threatened the eastern freight and migration routes to Utah in both 1863 and 1864. Many emigrants were routed through Canada to avoid troubles.[31] The multimillion-dollar freight business had Utah's entrepreneurs equally concerned. As a consequence, freighting from California increased and new considerations were given to that route for possible Mormon emigration.[32]

Very much a part of the milieu of 1864, for the Mormon leaders, was the discovery of gold and silver on their southern borders. General Patrick Edward Connor had been outspoken about his interest in Utah's mineral wealth and sought openly to promote its development.

36

Gold discoveries in this region of the Colorado had not only brought miners into the area, but had also expanded steam navigation on the river. George A. Johnson's steamers regularly visited Mojave Valley. By 1864, Samuel Adams began promoting another steam navigation company to be supported by Califoria merchants.[33]

Thus a number of factors came to focus on the region in the fall of 1864. Brigham Young had visited the cotton mission that summer. He knew firsthand that the southern Saints must be helped. General Connor had sent Lt. George F. Price to survey a new road between Camp Douglas and Fort Mojave on the Colorado River. Price reported back in July somewhat optimistically that a good route had been found via Clover and Meadow valleys in southeastern Nevada, areas which later proved rich in minerals.[34]

In August 1864, the *Daily Telegraph* reported that a James Ferry had located a landing in Circle Valley on the Colorado between Boulder Canyon on the east and Vegas Wash to the west. Ferry believed the river navigable to that point; but equally important, his route from Circle Valley avoided the terrible Virgin Hill between the Virgin River and Mormon Mesa.[35]

At the October conference, Apostle Erastus Snow's plea for the Cotton Mission came in this context. The assembled Saints voted to help in response to the request of Heber C. Kimball. In support of the action, Brigham Young offered to go himself if the conference wanted him to; and should he go, "he would soon have steamboats passing up the Colorado River."[36]

He also alluded to the new route for emigrating Saints into Zion because problems in "our once happy nation" would require it.[37]

But instead of President Young going south, "100 men of wealth" were selected either to go themselves or finance substitutes who would go for them. While few of these "men of wealth" actually went south, they, including President Young, Heber C. Kimball, William Jennings, William Godby, Hiram Clawson (merchants) and others, met on October 31 to organize the Deseret Mercantile Association.[38] Its purposes were threefold: to promote steam navigation of the Colorado River for freight and emigrants; to build a Mormon warehouse at its high point of navigation; and to establish interval settlements along the lower Virgin River between St. George and the landing. Consideration was also given to the potential for shipping sugar from Mormon plantations in the Sandwich Islands to Zion by way of the river.[39]

Needless to say, when news of the new venture reached St. George, the Saints there speculated on what migration through their community would mean. One true believer built a hotel to receive the travelers when they came.[40] Other Saints placed orders for goods with William Hardy's agents for delivery at Hardyville.

Meanwhile in Salt Lake City, the Deseret Mercantile Association selected Anson Call to choose a site and build a warehouse, to superintend a road to it, and to select at least two sites capable of supporting between fifty and two hundred families.[41] Call seemed to sense the need for immediate action, especially if they were to be ready for freight orders by early spring. Leaving Salt Lake City on November 15, 1864, he reached St. George nine days later, where he recruited the services of Jacob Hamblin and four others.

The small party left with pack animals for the lower Virgin, where Call selected the first settlement site at Beaver Dam (Millersburg, now Littlefield, Arizona).[42] The expedition continued west to the confluence of the Muddy, where a second larger settlement site was chosen. Their route turned down the Virgin to Echo Wash, up its course, across the divide into the upper drainage of Callville Wash, and south to the Colorado River, where Call selected a landing site for a warehouse one-quarter mile below the wash on the river's north bank. Call noted the bareness of the area they had passed through, especially the last twenty miles between the Virgin and Colorado rivers; however, he speculated that water for irrigating some 200 acres could be taken out upriver about one mile above the warehouse.[43]

It should be noted at this point that Call's route to the river was the same as that proposed by James Ferry earlier that summer. It seems that Call and Hamblin knew exactly where they were going, and no river reconnaissance was undertaken.

After selecting the site, the party continued west to the Great Bend, detouring up Vegas Wash to mail a report to President Horace Eldredge of the Deseret Mercantile Association. Call then continued south along the west bank of the river to Mojave Valley and Hardyville. Here he placed an order for supplies needed to build the warehouse. They were to be delivered at the site early in January 1865.[44]

The explorers returned to the site where Lyman Hamblin and James David were left to begin "digging the foundations for the warehouse."

Call's return route provided new exploration up the Colorado River around Boulder Canyon, up a wash north into the drainage of Echo Wash, and onto the Virgin River below the Salt Mountain.

From the settlement site (St. Thomas), the party explored eastward, through St. Thomas Gap, south of the Virgin Mountains into Grand Wash, up the Grand Wash Fault onto the Colorado Plateau and the "high mountains south of St. George," and then on into the city. For pack animals the route in late December was no challenge. However, Call's claim that the route could be put in good condition for $6,000 was quite unrealistic.[45] There is not yet a road in good condition through the area.

Once in St. George, Anson Call immediately set about to organize "laborers, mechanics, supplies and everything necessary to facilitate the erection of a warehouse without delay," which he expected to cost between twenty and thirty thousand dollars.[46] Supporters in Salt Lake City also seemed to sense an urgency. Stonemasons left for St. George by December 14. Settlers were organized under the leadership of Thomas Smith and Henry W. Miller and assigned to settle at St. Thomas and Millersburg respectively.

On December 28, settlers and workers joined forces enroute from St. George to the lower Virgin. Some road building was required for the wagons, so Call pushed ahead to begin work immediately. His two young foundation diggers, having run short of food, were met coming back. Call reached the landing early in January. The stonemasons arrived on January 13. William Hardy reached the site with his river barge a day later. He spoke optimistically about steamers and freighting possibilities for the landing, believing it to be accessible at least eight months of the year.[47] Hardy also filed on one of the lots in the Callville townsite.

The workmen proceeded with dispatch. Within twenty-seven days the large structure was nearly ready for a roof. Call asked the Indians to be on the alert for the steamer expected any day with roofing materials. They reported excitedly one day that they had discovered a "steamer track," which under closer scrutiny proved to have been made by one of Lt. Edward F. Beale's camels loose in the area. When Call and most of the crew left the landing on February 18, all hands were generally optimistic. A steamer was expected soon,[48] and they had built well. The warehouse still stood in 1934 when the waters of Lake Mead covered it.

Utah leaders were providing other support. On December 23, 1864, Brigham Young had written to Territorial Delegate J. F. Kinney asking that Congress "grant us about two degrees on one side or the other side of the river, to the Gulf of California, or to the boundary of the United States in that direction. This addition to our territory would give us an outlet on the western ocean as we need."[49] Suffice it to say Judge Kinney did not succeed with Congress. Even Territorial Governor James D. Doty asked for a memorial to Congress to add that area along the Virgin and Muddy rivers to Utah.[50] His and Brigham Young's proposals would come back to haunt them, for it was Utah that later lost lands to neighboring states.

While initially Brigham Young's and other Mormon merchants' support for the project had been strong, that situation changed dramatically in March of 1865. What happened? We know that Brigham Young had planned a trip as far south as the Colorado landing as late as January 31, 1865,[51] since letters to William Dame and Erastus Snow asked for teams and supplies for the trip. However, a second letter dated March 2 cancelled the trip. Why? If Call left the landing on February 18, he could have been in Salt Lake City by March 1. By that date it was becoming obvious that the national crisis was coming to an end, and that the freighting season from the east would likely be successful. It is believed that Anson Call must have said something to Brigham Young that changed his mind. In his March 2 letters to Dame and Snow, Young alluded to the late storms as a factor in canceling the trip.[52]

During January and February, Samuel Adams and Captain James Trueworthy were attempting to steam the *Esmeralda* upriver to the new landing. They reached the upper portions of Black Canyon above Roaring Rapids in late February, where they were only about twenty-eight miles from the new warehouse. However, at this point, according to Adams, they met persons from Callville who claimed that the Mormons had abandoned the landing. While Anson Call and crews had departed on the eighteenth, three men were left to receive the goods. As a result of this report, Trueworthy turned back to Eldorado Landing.[53] Again, what happened? Adams, who, with Captain Trueworthy, made his way overland to Salt Lake City, later reported that a letter from "interested parties" on the river had caused Call to "abandon the landing."[54] To date those details have not come to light, nor have the identities of the persons from Callville who reported that the Mormons had abandoned it.

Once in Salt Lake City, Adams and Trueworthy tried to drum up support for their steamer freight line on the Colorado River. Mormons expressed interest but gave no financial support. Judge Elias Smith noted at their April 13 meeting that "the 'Iron Horse' would soon be moving across the plains," anyway.[55] His comments reflected the changed attitude. The Civil War was over and the end of the nation not yet. Whether or not Call actually talked with Adams and Trueworthy has not been determined. At least neither party mentioned such an exchange, even though Call was in Davis County for several weeks while they were in Salt Lake City.

As one assigned to develop the route, Call's behavior is baffling. Apparently, while north (March to April) he generated several orders for goods, hoping thereby to test the route that season (1865).[56] As a result, he and his wife Mary Bowen returned south, reaching the landing on May 9. Call hoped the steamer *Cocopah* would soon arrive with roofing materials and with merchandise for William Jennings.[57] When Call learned that the *Cocopah* had stopped at Hardyville, he went himself to Eldorado Canyon. From what he heard, Call believed Hardy was sabotaging the new landing, desiring that all upriver freight come through his own place in Mojave Valley.[58] At this same time, Anson Call filed on 160 acres of land upriver from the landing about one mile, apparently the area he had earlier suggested could be irrigated from the Colorado River.[59] He then returned to the warehouse where he and Mary remained until mid-June, before abandoning the site.

The Mormon freight experiment had failed. Later uses of the landing did involve a few Mormons, but Gentile initiative and resources were the moving forces primarily. No doubt Call was very disappointed and frustrated. He never returned to Call's Landing. Apparently it was his son, Anson B. Call, whom Murl Emery boated to the spot in 1934 as the waters of Lake Mead were just reaching to the foundations of the warehouse.[60]

Before analyzing the significance of Call's effort, another important account of Mormon exploration and Call's Landing should be reviewed. One of the urgent needs anticipated by Mormon leaders in October 1864 was another route for emigrant Saints into Zion. To determine whether Colorado River emigration was feasible, George W. Brimhall was asked to take his wife and young family and try the route in reverse, that is, to make the trip from Utah Valley to Call's landing.

Responding to George A. Smith's request, Brimhall loaded his wife and six children (the oldest, George H., being but twelve at the time) into a covered wagon and joined other missionaries enroute to the Muddy River. Spring snows and rains hampered their progress as far south as Cedar City, but two weeks later they were sweating it out along the Virgin River. By the time they reached the Muddy and the St. Thomas settlement in late May of 1865, Brimhall's family was weary and he was worried. With only a few days' rest, Brimhall's family continued downriver.[61]

Writing in 1889, twenty-four years later, Brimhall related the events. First of all, he feared he would lose his family in that "burnt" country. When they reached "Poison Springs" in Echo Wash (probably Bitter Springs), they camped for the night. About dusk, Anson Call's party came in from the landing and camped below them a short distance. Apparently there was little exchange that evening. The next morning Brimhall found his oxen were too sick to move. When he contacted Call he discovered that three of Call's horses had died during the night and Call could not help him. Brimhall related that he blessed his oxen, and when they were able to travel he began his return to St. Thomas. George H. ran ahead to get water for the family, and they survived the very hazardous trip back.[62]

Still, Brimhall felt he must get to the landing in order to fulfill his mission call. So he, Elijah Elmore, and his thirteen-year-old son set out again with a team of young horses and a buggy. After a very difficult climb, they descended Callville Wash to the warehouse. Brimhall could see absolutely no redeeming features in the area or the landing.

While there, he and Elmore met three gentiles—O. D. Gass, James Ferry and William Cowan. These men convinced Brimhall that they, not the Mormons, owned the land and the minerals at the landing. A search of Mojave County records revealed that William Cowan had filed on 160 acres at the landing on May 5, 1865, some eleven days before Call filed on his land.[63] Brimhall and Elmore returned to St.

Thomas, happy to be rid of the river. In time Brimhall returned to Spanish Fork, reported to George A. Smith on his findings, and asked to be released from his mission to the Muddy.[64] His is a dramatic story but his impact somewhat anticlimactic, since the Mormons had in the main already abandoned the warehoue and landing.

Mormon mission emphasis soon shifted to possession of the land, to keeping out the gentiles, and to raising cotton, which appeared to have some promise.

Locally, Mormons did renew their interest in the river with the arrival of the steamer *Esmeralda* at Callville in October 1866. In 1867, Erastus Snow and other St. George leaders speculated on a better, shorter route to the Colorado River via Grand Wash. As a result, Jesse W. Crosby, Henry W. Miller, and Jacob Hamblin rowed a skiff downstream from the Grand Canyon to Callville.[65] While theirs was not the first exploration of that portion of the Colorado (James Ferry, O. D. Gass, and others had been through it in 1864), theirs was the best account of it until John Wesley Powell covered it in 1869, after exploring the canyons of the Colorado.

In spite of many setbacks, the cotton missionaries tried to remain on the Muddy. However, Indian raids, political uncertainty, and double taxation became too heavy a pioneering burden even for these Mormons. Brigham Young finally made his promised trip to the Colorado River in March of 1870.[66] In anticipation of his arrival, Bishop James Leithead and other men had built a barge to ferry President Young's wagon across the river so that he could explore further south. But when Young saw the Colorado River area, he had seen enough. He announced shortly afterwards that if the Muddy Mission Saints wanted to leave they could as long as they all went.[67] That vote came in December of 1870, and with it the Mormon tenure ended. A few years later, polygamous and United Order Mormons would claim the area, and survive.

What can one say about the Mormon venture onto the Colorado River in 1864–65? There are a number of valid observations to be noted. First of all, Mormon leaders obviously were influenced in their decisions by a variety of current circumstances and factors as they saw them. Almost coincidentally they had moved into Utah's Dixie and found there a mild climate which suggested that their plan for economic self-sufficiency could flourish. Their expectations for cotton growing, however, were unrealistic since they misinterpreted the Civil War and miscalculated its impact on them. Namely, the war was over before significant amounts of cotton were produced; hence, Utah producers again had to compete with the national market. The transcontinental railroad soon made Salt Lake City more accessible to Southern cotton growers than to the Virgin River producers. Even the cotton factory at Washington, Utah, was a post-Civil War product, and was always a far from lucrative venture for Dixie Mormons.

The Colorado River was at best only marginally navigable. Both Mormons and gentiles erred here in their speculations. But Mormon leaders again miscalculated when in 1865 they assumed that immigrants, and freight, would have to come via other than the eastern routes. No evidence of prescience of foreknowledge appears in their behavior as it related to the Colorado River venture in 1864–65.

The Mormons did move expeditiously on the warehouse and the landing. Anson Call wasted no time in launching his project, and he built well enough. However, the facts indicate that he (perhaps more correctly, the Mormons) failed to develop a landing at the high point of navigation on the Colorado River. No steamer reached Callville under Mormon domain. Nor for that matter was Callville the high point of river navigation, since steamers two decades later pushed up through Boulder Canyon to Bonelli's Ferry at the mouth of the Virgin River. However, Call's biggest fiasco seems to have been his building of a warehouse on property claimed legally by William Cowan.

Lest this summary seem too hard on Call, it is apparent that the project's failure was assured without this last fiasco. Mormons simply went there with too few means and for the wrong reasons in 1864–65.

But then Mormons are not the only ones who have failed or who have miscalculated. And they do have many successes to proclaim proudly. Yet there are aspects of this experience that ought to be given some pause. In their efforts to settle the west the Mormon leadership often ignored the sufferings of the colonists sent out. Brimhall states that he nearly lost his family, though he did not. However, other cotton missionaries did lose children and loved ones. Yet within six years (after President Young finally visited the area), the mission was abandoned. One can understand a former settler summarizing his years on the Muddy by saying, "Well, I guess we got experience."[68]

These Colorado River ventures suggest that there were for Mormon leaders in Utah between 1850 and 1870 several premises which they used in making decisions. We have noted the current issues. But in addition, Mormons and their leaders seemed to presume that God ruled in the universe, that life and history were, in effect, an unfolding of his will, his divine plan. Consequently, what was happening could be interpreted as God's will. The Civil War was in fact the judgment of God on a wicked nation that had persecuted his Saints. It was this frame of reference that caused several major miscalculations in the Mormon move to Callville.

There is another significant facet to this view. For the faithful, not only was history an unfolding of God's will, but Church leaders were viewed as the ones who understood these things best. Leaders were believed to be inspired, so that what they asked the Saints to do was seen as God's will for the members. One consequence for many cotton missionaries was extreme sacrifice, both economically and in loss of loved ones.

And how were they to judge the situation? Anson Call was certainly faithful to the end of his mission, maintaining as late as 1867 that the landing was a viable route for freight into Utah.[69] Another faithful stalwart was Bishop James Leithead who held out until 1871 only to settle in Long Valley above Kanab—in another remote and generally forbidding region. He finally moved to the Big Horn Basin in Wyoming early in the 1900s and died there about a decade later. On the other hand, George W. Brimhall, while faithful in performing a dangerous mission to explore the route for family migration, refused to remain on the Muddy River, which he hated. Rather, he returned to Utah Valley and its superior options for him and his family. His son, George H. Brimhall, in time became president of Brigham Young University.

For some of these Mormons, the issue was not one of options, but whether or not one would be faithful. In a man like Jacob Hamblin, the faith rationale is carried to its logical extension. On several occasions Hamblin saw and reported what he believed was supposed to be there, not what in fact was. Many of his observations about Lt. Ives's *Explorer* in 1858 were neither astute nor accurate. In 1876, Brigham Young assigned him to explore a route for the Mormon settlers on the Little Colorado River from St. George south and west across the Colorado River below the Grand Canyon and then southeast to the settlement sites. He reported back to the St. George conference that the route was one "sea of grass" all the way.[70] Travelers that next season did not agree at all. Another event in 1864 seems to explain Hamblin's attitudes even better. With the announcement that Mormons planned to establish a warehouse at the high point of navigation of the Colorado River, Hamblin, with others, appears to have projected that since the Virgin River at their doorstep near St. George emptied into the Colorado, it also should be navigable. As a result, Hamblin and crew launched their skiff *Virgin Adventurer* south of town to try the river. With dedication they eventually maneuvered to the narrows (through which the new I-15 now passes), but when the water disappeared underground, Hamblin's party gave up and returned to St. George overland.[71]

These exploration experiences also reveal situations that affect the Church leader in his roles. If he sees his work as God's will and his decisions as "inspired," then it is difficult for him to argue about their outcome, whether it is the institutional impact or its meaning to the individuals involved. Regarding the latter aspect, it would appear that leaders were often calloused or immune to the trials and hardships of specific people, especially those who had no voice in the councils. But then perhaps that condition is more an authoritative rather than a religious quality in the situation of leadership.

Therefore, it is necessary that historians look at the actions of religious leaders and measure them as one would any othe leader. While the historian as historian may not determine whether or not God inspired Mormon leaders in their ventures onto the lower Colorado River, he can look at their actions and judge them for what they were—failure, success, judicious, prescient, or otherwise. It is obvious that the decisions of Brigham Young and his associates relative to this area evolved according to available data. Some of it was accurate, some of it erroneous, and much of it pure pioneer-frontier speculation. Their decisions and the consequences of them reflect that mixture.

46

Notes

1. "A letter from Thomas L. Kane to Horace Greeley—being an abstract of the Original Description which induced M[ormon]s to settle in the Basin," Oscar O. Winther, *The Private Papers and Diary of Thomas Leiper Kane, a friend of The Mormons* (San Francisco: Gelber-Lilienthal, Inc., 1937), p. 7.

2. Mormon Battalion men reported on the river in November 1846, when they crossed at the Gila Junction. See "Journal of Robert S. Bliss, with the Mormon Battalion," *Utah Historical Quarterly* 4 (July 1931); and Henry W. Bigler, "Extracts from the Journal of Henry W. Bigler," *Utah Historical Quarterly* 5 (April 1932).

3. Ray M. Reeder, "The Mormon Trail: A History of the Salt Lake to Los Angeles Route" (Ph.D. diss., Brigham Young University, 1966), pp. 240–50.

4. LDS Journal History, March 9, 1849.

5. Parley P. Pratt, *The Autobiography of Parley P. Pratt* (New York: Russell Brothers, 1874), pp. 408–10.

6. George H. Derby, *Topographical Reports* (San Francisco: California Historical Society, 1933), pp. 61–62.

7. LDS Journal History, October 23, 1851.

8. Brigham Young, "Fifth General Epistle," *Millennial Star* 13(December 10, 1851): 209.

9. Captain Lorenzo Sitgreaves, *Report of an Expedition Down the Zuni and Colorado Rivers* (Washington: Robert Armstrong, Public Printers, 1853), pp. 4–20.

10. Lieutenant Amiel W. Whipple, *Reports of Exploration and Survey to Ascertain the Most Practicable and Economic Route for a Railroad from the Mississippi River to the Pacific Ocean, 1853–1854* (Washington: A. O. P. Nichols, Printer, 1856), pp. 100–120.

11. *Deseret News*, December 14, 1854.

12. Andrew Jensen, comp., "The History of the Las Vegas Mission," *Nevada State Historical Society Papers, 1925–1926* 5(1926):119–285.

13. Ibid., pp. 238–39.

14. *Deseret News*, October 1, 1855.

15. Andrew Love Neff, *History of Utah* (Salt Lake City: Deseret News Press, 1940), p. 134.

16. Thomas D. Brown, "Journal for the Southern Indian Mission," typescript, Utah State Historical Society, pp. 120–25.

17. Jensen, "Las Vegas Mission," pp. 270–76.

18. Lynn R. Bailey, ed., "Lt. Sylvester Mowry's Report on His March in 1855 from Salt Lake City to Fort Tejon," *Arizona and the West* 7(Winter 1865):329–45.

19. Neff, *History of Utah*, pp. 805–6.

20. Juanita Brooks, *The Mountain Meadows Massacre* (Norman: University of Oklahoma Press, 1962), p. 22.

21. Jacob Hamblin, "Jacob Hamblin Journals, 1854, 1858, 1869, 1874" (Typescript, Utah State Historical Society), pp. 28–30.

22. Joseph C. Ives, *Report Upon The Colorado River of The West* (Washington: Government Printing Office, 1861), pp. 39–40.

23. Hamblin, "Jacob Hamblin Journals."

24. Amasa M. Lyman, "Journal Number 16", typescript, Brigham Young University Library, pp. 95–105.

25. *Deseret News*, July 21, 1858.

26. Jensen, "The History of the Las Vegas Mission," p. 381.

27. Andrew Karl Larson, *I Was Called to Dixie* (Salt Lake City: Deseret News Press, 1964).

28. Ibid.

29. Doctrine and Covenants 87.

30. Leonard J. Arrington, *The Great Basin Kingdom* (Cambridge: Harvard University Press, 1958), p. 220.

31. "Conference Report, October 8, 1864," *Millennial Star* 26(December 3, 1864):768–69.

32. Reeder, "The Mormon Trail."

33. Francis Leavitt, "The Influence of the Mormon People in the Settlement of the Clark County" (MA thesis, University of Nevada, Reno, 1934), p. 63.

34. "Report of Lt. Price," *Daily Union Vedette* (Salt Lake City), July 25, 1864.

35. *Salt Lake Daily Telegraph*, August 27, 1864.

36. "Conference Report, October 8, 1864," *Millennial Star* 26(December 3, 1864):769–70.

37. Ibid. See also "Letter of Brigham Young, December 5, 1864," *Millennial Star* 27(January 21, 1864):41; "Letter of George Q. Cannon to Daniel H. Wells and Brigham Young, Jr., December 7, 1864," *Millennial Star* 27(February 4, 1864):78; and "Letter of Wilford Woodruff, January 16, 1865," *Millennial Star* 27(April 9, 1865), p. 219.

38. *Salt Lake Daily Telegraph*, November 2, 1864.

39. Leonard J. Arrington, "Inland to Zion: Mormon Trade on the Colorado River, 1864-1867," *Arizona and The West* 7(Autumn 1966):245.

40. Charles L. Walker, "Diary of Charles Lowell Walker," Dixie College Library, St. George, Utah.

41. *Salt Lake Daily Telegraph*, November 9, 1864. See also "Life and Record of Anson Call" p. 71, Utah State Historical Society.

42. *Deseret News,* January 18, 1864.

43. Ibid.; and Salt Lake *Daily Telegraph*, January 2, 1865.

44. Ibid.

45. Ibid.; and January 16, 1865.

46. *Deseret News*, January 18, 1865.

47. *Salt Lake Daily Telegraph*, January 25, 1865.

48. ibid., March 18, 1865.

49. Brigham Young to Judge J. F. Kinney, Washington, D.C., December 23, 1864, Church Archives, Historical Department, The Church of Jesus Christ of Latter-day Saints, Salt Lake City, Utah (hereafter cited as LDS Church Archives).

50. *Deseret News,* December 14, 1864.

51. Brigham Young to William H. Dame, January 31, 1865, LDS Church Archives; also Brigham Young to William H. Dame, March 2, 1865; and Brigham Young to Erastus Snow, March 2, 1865, LDS Church Archives.

52. Ibid.

53. *Salt Lake Daily Telegraph*, March 27, 1867.

54. Ibid.

55. *Millennial Star* 27(June 10, 1865):365–66.

56. *Deseret News*, May 5, 1865.

57. Anson Call to George A. Smith, from Callville, Arizona, May 24, 1865, LDS Church Archives.

58. *San Francisco Evening Bulletin*, July 8, 1865.

59. "Pre-emption Claim of A. Call," Mojave County Misc. Documents, Book 1, p. 10, Recorder's Office, Kingman, Arizona.

60. Interview with Murl Emery, Nelson, Nevada, March 22, 1968.

61. Report of George W. Brimhall to George A. Smith, December 10, 1865, LDS Church Archives.

62. George W. Brimhall, *Workers of Utah* (Provo: Privately published, 1889), pp. 45–49.

63. Report of George W. Brimhall to George A. Smith. See also "Preemption Claim of W. Cowan," Mojave County Misc. Documents, Book 1, p. 11, Recorder's Office, Kingman, Arizona. The witness to Cowan's claim was James Ferry.

64. Ibid.

65. *Deseret News*, July 3, 1867. Members of the expedition also included James Andrus, Ira Hatch, Erastus Snow, and David Cameron.

66. *Deseret News*, March 19, 1870, and April 13, 1870.

67. Arabell Hafner, *100 Years on The Muddy* (Springville: Art City Publishing Co., 1967), pp. 80–81.

68. Ibid.

69. *Daily Union Vidette*, November 23, 1867.

70. *Deseret News* February 28, 1877; and Pearson H. Corbett, *Jacob Hamblin the Peacemaker* (Salt Lake City: Deseret Book Co., 1952), pp. 329–96.

71. *Deseret News*, March 1, 1865.

Defunct Mormon Settlements: 1830–1930

Lynn A. Rosenvall

During the latter half of the nineteenth century, members of The Church of Jesus Christ of Latter-day Saints established nearly 500 settlements in the West, in an area covering seven states and stretching from Mexico to Canada. This colonizing project has been extolled as being unusually successful; thus, one could easily gain the impression that all these settlements are still in existence. Moreover, almost all books and articles that describe western ghost towns fail to list any of the Mormon communities that have been deserted. These publications might note ghost towns within the Mormon region, but invariably these towns are defunct Utah mining centers, such as Frisco, Silver Reef, and Mercur.[1] But then, since extinct settlements often fail to leave any evidence of their existence, it is not surprising that many persons are unaware of this facet of Mormon history.

In this article, defunct Mormon settlements are enumerated and then classified according to "reason for failure." Lastly, these "reasons" are analyzed. The year 1900 has been recognized as a practical terminal date for Mormon colonization, and in this study only those settlements that were *founded* prior to 1900 are included.[2] The year 1930, however, was selected as the closing date for defunct settlements. Thus, only those settlements that *failed* before 1930 are enumerated and analyzed. The reasons for selecting this year are threefold: (1) all of the more important defunct settlements failed prior to 1930, (2) the period of thirty years from 1900 to 1930 provides a potential "failure zone" for settlements that were founded toward the end of the nineteenth century, and (3) many small rural settlements in the United States exodus from rural to urban centers. Thus, the use of 1930 as the terminal date helped eliminate from consideration the Mormon settlements that suffered this form of demise and which could contaminate an analysis of settlement failures unique to Mormon colonization.[3]

Research on all Mormon settlements indicates that 69 have ceased to exist out of the 497 communities (13.9 percent) that were founded in the United States during the period of 1847 to 1900.[4] When the communities that were founded in the Midwest, Canada, and Mexico are included, the failure rate jumps to 16.4 percent or 88 settlements out of the total of 537 settlements.

These failure rates may appear to be high in light of the careful attention the Mormons gave to locating their settlements. But, on the other hand, when one considers the uninviting environment of many of these settlements and the debilitating external factors that their inhabitants faced, one can begin to understand why the failure percentages are so high.

Classifications

The 88 defunct Mormon settlements can be readily divided into two major classes: (1) settlements that failed because of pressures from outside forces over which the Mormons had little or no control, and (2) settlements that ceased to exist of their own volition and not under pressure from external forces. The first class has been entitled "External Factors" and has been separated into several subclasses, comprising such factors as Indian conflicts, the coming of Johnston's army ("Utah War"), religious conflicts, and the Mexican Revolution. The second major class or group of settlements was abandoned, in general, because of factors that can be linked to the environment. This class has been labeled "Environmental Factors" and divided into subclasses representing such factors as floods, inadequate water supply, and poor location.

The following is an analysis of the communities within each of the two classes—when they were founded, where they were located, and why they ceased to exist. Other information, where applicable, is included to help with the analysis. Some settlements failed for more than one reason. The reason given in this analysis is the one that appears to be the prime cause of failure. Some settlements ceased to exist merely because their inhabitants moved away one by one for various reasons until the community was completely abandoned.

External Factors

This class of defunct settlements is, by far, the smaller of the two classes—26 failures out of 497 settlements or 5.2 percent. If the defunct settlements from the Midwest, Canada, and Mexico that belong in the same class are included, the failure rate increases from 5.2 percent to 7.8 percent (42 out of the new total of 537 settlements). All of the settlements in the Midwest and most of those in Mexico were abandoned for reasons that are included under this class, hence the large increase in the failure rate.

Indian Conflicts

Even though it was Mormon policy to "feed the Indians rather than fight them," many communities still suffered appreciable losses at the hands of the Indians. Some 45 settlements were vacated for one year or more because of Indian conflicts. Most of these communities were abandoned during the fateful years of the Walker (1853–54) and Black Hawk (1865–66) Indian wars.[5] The majority of these settlements—36 out of 45—were vacated for periods of up to twelve years and then resettled after the Indian hostilities had subsided, but nine were never resettled. (see Table 1).[6]

These nine settlements were located in the area of the present-day state of Utah, except for Fort Limhi in the Salmon River area of Idaho, and Forest Dale and Tuba City in Arizona (see Fig. 1). With the exception of the Elk Mountain Indian mission, all of the settlements in this category located in Utah were vacated during the Black Hawk Indian War. Many other Utah settlements were abandoned a decade earlier during the Walker Indian War, but all of these communities were only temporarily vacated and later resettled.

It should be noted that Northrop, Zion, and Dalton were all located in the Virgin River area of southern Utah and that these communities had experienced the vicissitudes of that river. Poor location, therefore, could also have been a contributing factor in the decision not to reoccupy these particular settlements. Tuba City and Forest Dale were vacated much later than their Utah counterparts (1903 and 1882 respectively), but these settlements were also founded several years later than the Utah communities. In addition, Indian problems in Arizona continued to occur some two to three decades after such conflicts had ceased in Utah.

TABLE 1

DEFUNCT MORMON SETTLEMENTS (EXTERNAL FACTORS)

Settlement[a]	State[b]	Year Founded	Year Failed[c]
Indian Conflicts			
Fort Limhi	Idaho	1855	1858
Elk Mountain	Utah	1855	1855
Mound City	Utah	1859	1866
Northrop	Utah	1862	1865
Zion	Utah	1862	1865
Dalton	Utah	1864	1866
Fort Sanford	Utah	1866	1867
Tuba City	Arizona	1873	1903
Forest Dale	Arizona	1878	1882
The "Utah War"			
Mormon Station	Nevada	1849	1857
San Bernardino	California	1851	1857
Fort Supply	Wyoming	1853	1857
Fort Bridger	Wyoming	1855	1857
Las Vegas	Nevada	1855	1857
Frankton	Nevada	1856	1857
Nevada Tax Problems			
Mill Point	Nevada	1865	1871
Simonsville	Nevada	1865	1871
Spring Valley	Nevada	1865	1871
Junction City	Nevada	1869	1871
West Point	Nevada	1869	1871
Religious Conflicts			
Pleasanton	New Mexico	1882	1889
Wilford	Arizona	1883	1885
Miscellaneous			
Mountain Dell	Utah	1858	1918
Pipe Springs	Arizona	1863	1920
Call's Landing	Nevada	1864	1869
Knightsville	Utah	1897	1930
Religious Conflicts in the Midwest			
Kirtland	Ohio	1831	1838

Far West	Missouri	1836	1839
Adam-ondi-Ahman	Missouri	1838	1839
Nauvoo	Illinois	1839	1846
Morley's Settlement	Illinois	1839	1846
Ramus	Illinois	1840	1846
Ambrosia	Iowa	1840	1846
Zarahemla	Iowa	1841	1846
Temporary Settlements in the Midwest			
Council Bluffs	Iowa	1846	1852
Garden Grove	Iowa	1846	1852
Mount Pisgah	Iowa	1846	1852
Winter Quarters	Nebraska	1846	1863
Mexican Revolution			
Colonia Diaz	Chihuahua	1885	1912
Galeana	Chihuahua	1895	1912
Colonia Morelos	Sonora	1900	1912
Colonia San Jose	Sonora	1905	1912

[a]The name given is the last name by which each settlment was known. Many of these settlements were founded under other names that have changed through the years. Some of these communities were reoccupied by non-Mormons and given different names.

[b]The state listed is the current state. Because of the several boundary changes that have taken place, many defunct settlements were once under the jurisdiction of other states or territories. For example, Mormon Station was originally in the Utah Territory, but that area is now part of Nevada. The location of each settlement is indicated in Figures 1 and 2. For maps showing the exact location of each defunct settlement, see Lynn A. Rosenvall, "Mormon Settlement Patterns: 1830–1900" (Ph.D. diss., University of California, Berkeley, 1972).

[c]Date settlement ceased to exist. It is difficult to assign an exact failure date to many of these settlements because they were vacated over a period of time. For some settlements the failure period could be before or after the date listed, or both. Some of these sites, such as Elk Mountain, San Bernardino, Mormon Station, and Las Vegas, were reoccupied in later years by other groups of people.

The "Utah War"

The coming of Johnston's army—an appellation given to the so-called Buchanan Expedition which was sent to Utah in 1857 by President James Buchanan—was a factor in the demise of several settlements.[7]

One of Brigham Young's defensive strategies in preparation for the coming of the "expedition" was to vacate the outlying settlements and

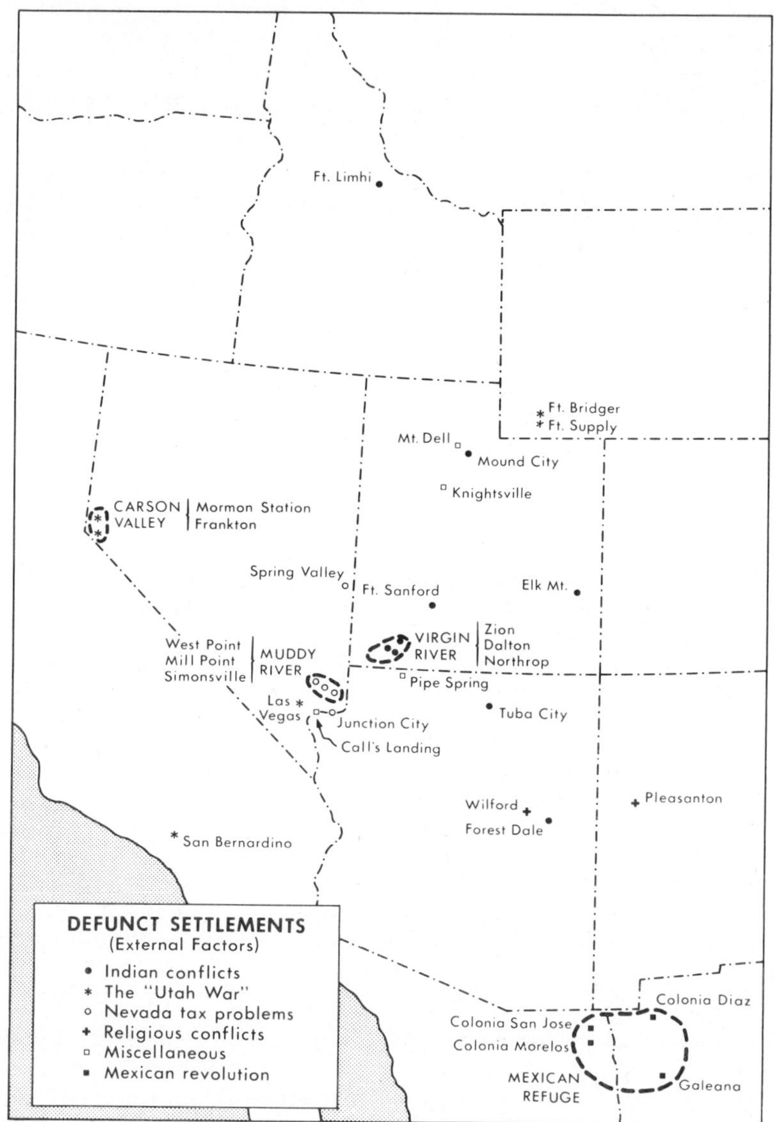

FIGURE 1

Defunct Mormon settlements (External Factors)

to bring all persons from these communities back to the center of the region (Salt Lake City and environs). As a further defensive maneuver, the Mormons vacated all their settlements located north of Salt Lake City; the plan was to destroy all the improvements in these settlements if the "expedition" became hostile.

In 1858, peace was again secured, and the northern settlements were subsequently resettled. The outlying settlements, however, were not reestablished. The Mormons feared that these remote communities could not be adequately defended because they were located too far from the center of the region. Also, the San Bernardino[8] and Carson Valley areas (Mormon Station and Frankton)[9] had experienced conflicts with non-Mormons and discouragement even before they were vacated in 1857.[10] It is highly probable that all of these outlying settlements would shortly have been vacated even if the "Utah War" had not occurred. Fort Supply and Fort Bridger were both burned to the ground by the Mormons, in the expectation that the destruction of these supply forts would impede the progress of Johnston's army. Las Vegas was almost abandoned prior to 1857 because of the failure in lead mining and problems with the Indians in the area.[11]

Nevada Tax Problems

The valley of the Muddy River, a tributary of the Virgin River in southeastern Nevada, was settled by Mormons in 1865. This area was at that time part of the territory of Utah, and the Muddy River settlements were to be way stations for the movement of emigrants and freight from California to Salt Lake City via the Colorado River.[12]

The Mormons also anticipated that this area would produce citrus fruit and cotton because of its warm climate and long growing season. But the Muddy Valley was not a desirable region to colonize. The area was somewhat removed from the closest settlements near St. George, and the Muddy River was undependable as a water source because it flooded readily and also because it was completely dry for part of each year.[13] Also, timber was scarce in the area, and the numerous tule swamps were breeding grounds for malaria-carrying mosquitoes.

Even with all these handicaps several settlements were established, and the settlers were beginning to see the fruits of their labors. Then, the fatal blow came in 1870 when a federal boundary survey revealed that they were no longer located in the territory of Utah but in the state of Nevada. Larson has explained the consequences of this situation as follows:

On February 15, 1869, the Utah Territorial Legislature created the Rio Virgin County out of the western part of Washington County. Previous to this time the Muddy settlers had paid their taxes, such as they were, to Washington County [southern Utah]. The tax was not high in the new county—at first only one-half of one per cent and later three-fourths—and since it could be paid in kind it was not at all burdensome. In 1866 the Congress of the United States took one full degree of territory from western Utah and Arizona and added it to Nevada. Thus without their consent the towns on the Muddy and those west and northwest of St. George (Panaca, Eagleville, Clover Valley, etc.) were placed in Nevada. This in itself was not serious; but what made it so for the Saints was the Nevada tax, which was about five times as high as the amount charged in Utah. This, too, could possibly have been met; but the hitch was that Nevada demanded payment in gold at the rate of three per cent plus a poll tax of $4 also payable in gold. The people on the Muddy simply did not have the gold to pay these taxes.[14]

After considering all the alternatives, the Mormons elected to vacate the Muddy River area. So, in February 1871, all the settlements were evacuated with most of the settlers moving to Long Valley in southern Utah (Kane County), an area that had been abandoned in 1866 because of Indian troubles. In the 1800s, three of these communities on the Muddy River were resettled by Mormons—Saint Thomas, Overton, and Saint Joseph.[15]

Spring Valley, a settlement north of the Muddy River, was also vacated in 1871 when the general exodus from Nevada took place. The nearby settlements of Eagle Valley and Panaca were not completely evacuated, some of the settlers choosing to remain and continue their holdings.

Religious Conflicts

The Mormons experienced few religious conflicts in the West, although some were heavily persecuted for practicing polygamy. Only two settlements, however, were abandoned because of these problems—Wilford, Arizona, and Pleasanton, New Mexico. Most of the inhabitants in both of these settlements were polygamists, and when the antipolygamy raids were instituted in the 1880s these persons moved to Mexico to escape arrest. Many other polygamist Mormons left for Mexico or Canada at this same time, but these two settlements appear to be the only ones that were completely abandoned because of religious conflicts.

Miscellaneous Conflicts

The settlements listed under this heading were vacated for reasons which were not uncommon for many areas of the United States. Mountain Dell, Utah (a few miles east of Salt Lake City), was vacated because a reservoir was built on that site; Pipe Springs, Arizona, was made part of a national monument in 1920; Call's Landing, Nevada, a settlement intended to be a transshipment point for goods shipped from southern California to Utah by way of the Colorado River, was abandoned in the late 1860s before fulfilling its planned purpose; and Knightsville, Utah, was vacated in the 1920s when the local mines were closed.

Religious Conflicts in the Midwest

All of the settlements founded in the Midwest were eventually vacated as a result of religious problems and were left by the Mormons to others. The settlements in Missouri were evacuated in 1839, whereas those in the Nauvoo region of Illinois were not abandoned until 1846. The latter expulsion forced the Mormons to seek refuge in the West.

Temporary Settlements in the Midwest

To expedite the movement of thousands of Mormons from the Midwest to their new haven in the West, temporary settlements were founded in Iowa and Nebraska. Three of these settlements—Mount Pisgah, Council Bluffs, and Garden Grove—were vacated in 1852 after most of the Mormons had been safely moved to Utah. Winter Quarters, however, continued until 1863 as the chief outfitting center for Mormon emigrants preparing for the last leg of their journey across the plains.

Mexican Revolution

From 1885 to 1905, several settlements were founded in the states of Sonora and Chihuahua in Mexico. This area was settled, at first, as a refuge for Mormon polygamists who had left the United States to escape arrest.[16] In 1887 and 1892, two of these settlements were abandoned for environmental reasons. But in 1912 the nine remaining settlements suffered from the changing fortunes of a Mexican revolution. All these communities were completely vacated except for Colonia Jua-

60

rez, which was only partly abandoned. Beginning in 1914, five of these communities were eventually resettled, but the other four settlements were never reoccupied.

Environmental Factors

Fully 43 Mormon settlements in the West ceased to exist because of "environmental factors" compared to the 26 failures listed under "external factors." These 43 defunct settlements represent 8.7 percent of the 497 communities founded in the United States during the period 1847–1900. In contrast, only three of the settlements founded in the Midwest, Canada, and Mexico fall into this class—one in Canada and two in Mexico. Adding these three to the total number of settlements does not appreciably affect the failure rate (46 out of 537 settlements or 8.6 percent).

This class of defunct settlements is possibly the more important of the two classes, because by analyzing these settlements one can begin to judge the ability of the Mormons to locate permanent settlements within some of the harsh environments of the arid West.

To most early observers the Mormons were foolhardy to attempt to make any settlements in the Great Basin and vicinity, let alone nearly 500 separate communities. But even before they arrived, the Mormons knew that these new areas would be challenging environments in which to settle; therefore, a great effort was made to gather all information that earlier explorers had written about the region.[17] When they reached the Great Salt Lake Valley, exploratory expeditions were sent out in several directions to get the "lay of the land." Moreover, from 1847 to 1864 at least 12 major exploring expeditions were made by the Mormons.[18] These explorations, coupled with numerous smaller excursions, enabled them to ascertain the nature of the country they were attempting to colonize. The plan of the Church was for settlements to be founded in light of this information and not on the personal whim of any individual or group; but in some instances individuals or groups did start their own settlements.[19]

How well the Mormons' colonizing efforts succeeded or did not succeed in the West is graphically illustrated in Figure 2. For each decade from 1847 to 1900, the number of settlements that were founded within each ten-year period—and that eventually failed for environmental reasons—is compared to the total number of settlements founded during the same decade. This ratio is expressed as a percentage and then plotted on the graph accordingly.

One might expect that most of the Mormon failures would occur during the first few years in the West, because they would have to learn about their new region by trial and error. But, surprisingly, there were no settlements founded during the first period (1847–49) that failed for reasons that could be linked to environment. The period with the highest failure rate was the decade of 1870–79, the time period when areas of the Colorado Plateau, mainly Arizona, were first settled. By 1870 the most desirable areas of the Mormon region were occupied, and only marginal spots remained to be colonized. Figure 3 also indicates that during the last decade of the nineteenth century the failure rate dropped to a low of 2.4 percent. It should be noted, however, that during this decade only three settlements were founded in the area with the highest failure rate—the area south of the state of Utah.

Floods

The Mormons were very careful to determine that each location they settled had sufficient water all year long to supply the anticipated populace. Still, one might suspect that the major reason for settlement failure in the semiarid and arid West would be inadequate water supply. But, paradoxically, the largest number of settlements failed because of an *excess* amount of water in the adjacent rivers during part of some years (see Table 2).

Flooding was not a major problem, in general, for the settlements situated along the Wasatch Front. But when the Mormons pushed south and attempted to establish settlements on the Colorado Plateau by using irrigation water from the tributaries of the Colorado River, they then encountered the problem of rivers readily overflowing their banks. As can be seen in Figure 3, all the settlements which were vacated because of floods were located along the tributary drainage of the Colorado River—the Virgin River, Johnson Wash, the Paria River, and the Fremont River in Utah; and the Little Colorado River in eastern Arizona. The flow of these rivers and streams can fluctuate greatly from day to day and even from year to year, and this is what caused the problem.[20]

Nearly all of the many settlements founded in these areas "struggled" at some time with these rivers. Dams built to impound and divert water for irrigation were time and time again destroyed by the sudden increases in the flow of water. Most of the settlements were able to "hold on" and repair the flood damage, but 16 settlements eventually were vacated because of the almost annual floods (see Table 2). The experiences of the communities along the Little Colorado River in Arizona are typical:

Every settlement along the Little Colorado River has known repeated troubles in maintaining its water supply. . . . [The river] is a treacherous stream at best, with

TABLE 2

**DEFUNCT MORMON SETTLEMENTS
(ENVIRONMENTAL FACTORS)**

Settle-ment[a]	State[b]	Year Founded	Year Failed[c]
		Floods	
Price	Utah	1858	1904
Tonaquint	Utah	1859	1862
Adventure	Utah	1860	1860*
Duncan's Retreat	Utah	1861	1891
Mountain Dell	Utah	1861	1900a
Shonesburg	Utah	1862	1893a
Paria	Utah	1865	1930
Scutumpah	Utah	1870	1879
Johnson	Utah	1871	1901*
Adairville	Utah	1873	1878
Obed	Arizona	1876	1878
Sunset	Arizona	1876	1888
Taylor	Arizona	1878	1878
Bloomington	Utah	1879	1930*
Caineville	Utah	1883	1909
Giles	Utah	1883	1910
		Poor Location	
Palmyra	Utah	1852	1856
Fort Saint Luke	Utah	1854	1855

63

Meadows	Arizona	1879	1886b
MacDonald	Arizona	1882	1885a
La Plata	New Mexico	1883	1889*
Nephi	Arizona	1887	1904*

Inadequate Water Supply

Clifton	Utah	1876	1896b
Georgetown	Utah	1886	1894a
Elephant	Utah	1887	1930b
Eastdale	Colorado	1889	1909

Miscellaneous

Morristown	Idaho	1863	1891
Brigham City	Arizona	1876	1881
Iosepa	Utah	1889	1917
Georgetown	Nevada	1898	1903

Canada and Mexico

Cave Valley	Chihuahua	1887	1900*
Colonia Oaxaca	Sonora	1892	1911
Caldwell	Alberta	1898	1911

---

[a] See footnote a, Table 1.

[b] See footnote b, Table 1.

[c] See footnote c, Table 1. The letter "a" following the date indicates that the settlement ceased to exist within a short period *after* the date listed; the letter "b" indicates that the demise took place within a short period *before* the date listed; and the asterisk (*) indicates that the date in only approximate, and the failure period could be before or after or both.

a broad channel that wanders at will through the alluvial country that melts like sugar or salt at the touch of water.

There are instances that stand out in this struggle for water. The first joint dam of Allen's Camp [later known as St. Joseph and Joseph City] and Obed cost the settlers $5000. It is told that 960 days work was done on the dam and 500 days more on the Allen ditch. This dam went down at the first flood, for it raised the water about twelve feet. Then, in the spring of 1867, another dam was built, a mile and a half upstream, and this again washed away. In 1879 the St. Joseph settlers sought a third damsite at LeRoux Wash, about two and a half miles west of the present Holbrook. In 1881 they spent much money and effort on the *plan to make a high dam at the site of the first construction, but this again was taken downstream by the river. In 1882, a pile dam was built across the river, and it was spoiled by floods. This dam generally was in use until 1891, but had to be repaired almost every year.... St. Joseph, as early as 1894, had completed its eighth dam across the river.*[21]

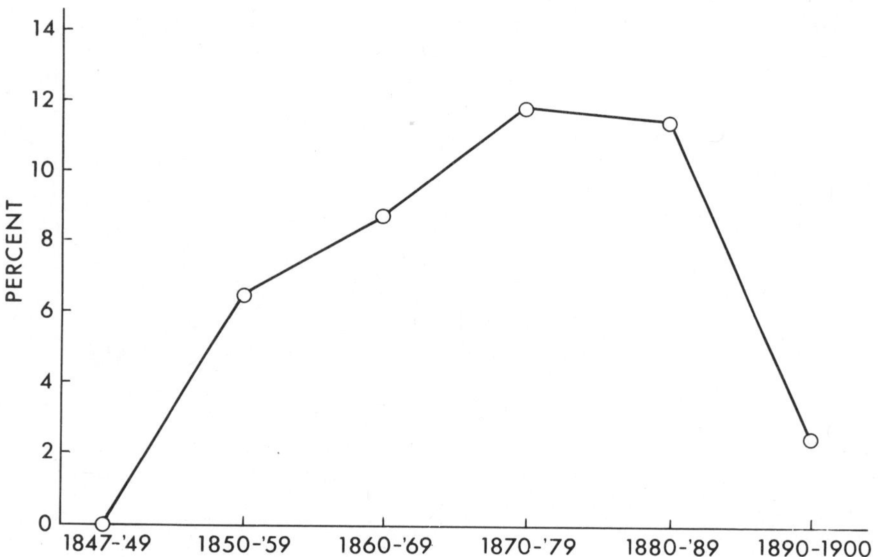

FIGURE 2

Total number of defunct Mormon settlements (Environmental Factors) compared to total number of settlements founded during the same decade. This ratio is expressed as a percentage.

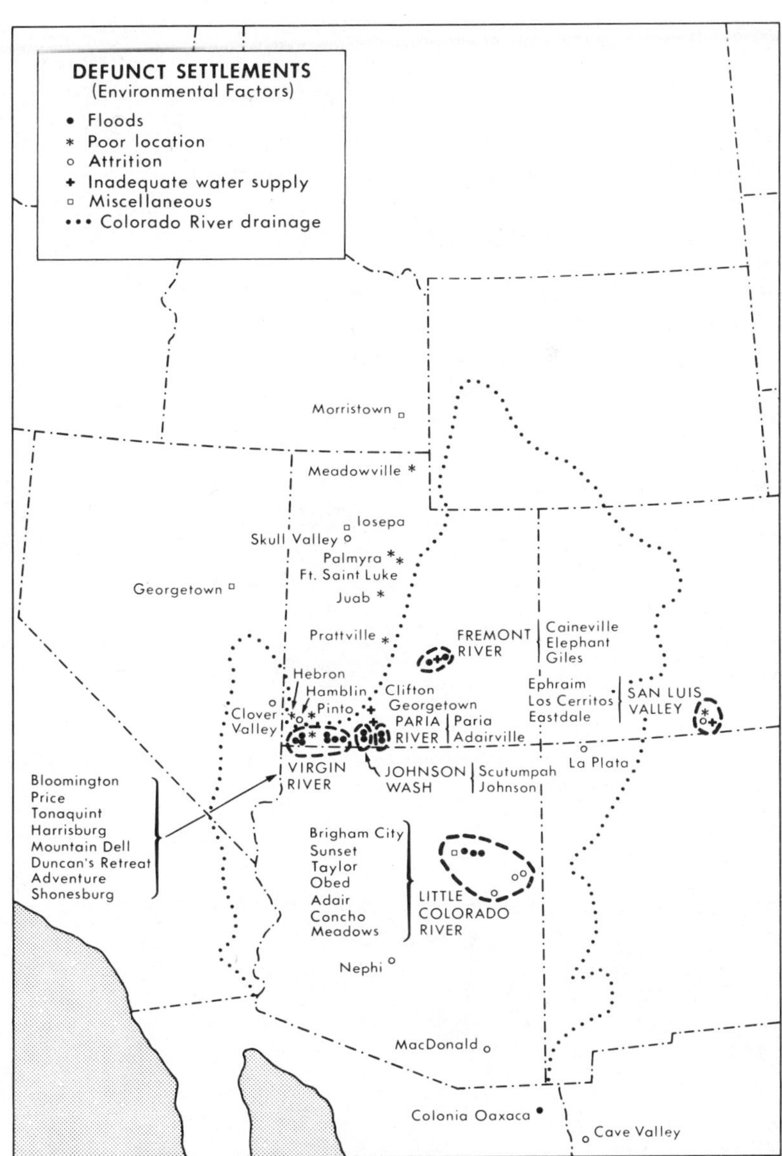

FIGURE 3

Defunct Mormon settlements (Environmental Factors)

66

Another area that experienced great flood damage was the Virgin River region of southern Utah. Larson has described some of their problems as follows:

The dam in the [Virgin] river was washed out twice in both 1857 and 1858. In 1859 when Apostle Franklin D. Richards and Joseph A. Young visited Washington [settlement four miles east of St. George] in midsummer, they found the group of colonists about ready to give up the struggle. Storms that season had been frequent, and their dams had been carried away three times. It was not that the floods were very large: a reasonably gusty freshet could do the damage. The troubles in rebuilding the structure overtaxed the strength of the few settlers who remained, and this with the malaria which most of these had to suffer just about convinced them that moving away was the only logical solution. Time spent in building dams in midsummer meant neglect of farm work, and work was necessary to get food to eat.

The year 1860 brought no change in the turbulence of the river. With each succeeding flood the channels grew a bit deeper and wider and harder to control. It took more brush, rocks, and trees to rebuild the dam, and with the exception of rock these materials were getting harder and harder to obtain.[22]

It is noteworthy that most of these settlements were vacated only after they had struggled with the water problem for several decades. The floods destroyed valuable farmland, and because many of these settlements were located in confined valleys or ravines the available land was very limited. When the available land was destroyed the settlements had to be abandoned.

Poor Location

Even with all the care and attention paid to the proper siting of settlements there were still nine communities with locations that proved to be undesirable. In most cases, it was not that the whole region or valley was unfit for occupancy, but rather that a settlement's paticular site was poor. The locations of these "poor" sites show no definite pattern. They occur in many different areas and were often surrounded by very successful communities. There were even four of these settlements located along the Wasatch Front.

These sites were undesirable for several reasons. For example, the residents of Meadowville in northern Utah, Palmyra in central Utah, and Ephraim in the San Luis Valley of Colorado all found that their locations were too low in relation to the surrounding terrain. When the settlers attempted to irrigate, the land drainage was inadequate and it became very swampy. The inhabitants of Meadowville moved to another site a few miles away, but eventually both sites were abandoned. The settlers at Palmyra solved their water problem by moving to nearby Spanish Fork, and the inhabitants of Ephraim transferred their homes to Manassa, a distance of only about five miles.

Limited or poor soil for growing crops was also a common complaint. And if the area of good soil was in short supply the settlements could not increase in size. This was a problem especially when the original settlers' children married and desired farms of their own. As was the case with the settlements noted above, most of these communities solved their soil problems by merely moving to a nearby settlement which had proven to be better situated. The inhabitants at Harrisburg moved to Leeds, and the settlers at Fort Saint Luke transferred to Spanish Fork, and most persons at Juab made new homes at Levan.

Pinto and Hebron, both located on the southern fringe of the Escalante Desert in southern Utah, were rather isolated with no other settlements within many miles. These two communities started new settlements within 15 miles of their old sites, which had proven to be in poor locations. The settlers at Pinto founded Newcastle and the inhabitants of Hebron transferred to a site they called Enterprise. Many of these poorly located communities toiled and struggled with their land for half a century or more before they "gave up" and sought a new site.

Attrition

Some ten settlements were vacated through the process of attrition; that is, over a period of several decades the population of these communities slowly decreased until the places ceased to exist as settlements. Most of these communities were located on the fringes of the Mormon region, especially in Arizona, and several were very isolated. These settlements had only small populations even at their peak; hence, it did not take long for them to "disappear from the map." Some of these settlements consisted of only a few families, and often their children would decide to seek homes in better locations. Within one generation it was possible for a community to be completely deserted.

In some areas, livestock grazing was often the best means of "living off the land." The large acreage required for animal grazing impeded the growth of these communities and often led to a decrease in population. Wanderlust was also a factor in the vacating of a few communities, since some settlers developed a pattern of "moving on" every few years as they sought for "greener pastures." For example, some individuals started at Salt Lake City and then moved to Iron County in southern Utah; later they shifted to the St. George area, and from there to Arizona or New Mexico. In later years their names can be found among the lists of settlers in the Mexican colonies. Note that almost all of the settlements listed under this heading were founded after 1870; in other words, they were founded after the most desirable areas in the Mormon region had already been colonized.

Inadequate Water Supply

Insufficient irrigation water, although it was *not* a major factor in settlement failure, forced four communities to be vacated. These settlements were predominantly located in the most arid parts of southern Utah. All of them were founded near the end of the nineteenth century after the better sites had been occupied and only marginal land remained for colonization. The water flow in the adjacent rivers, especially the Paria and Fremont rivers, was extremely erratic and undependable, and it was not uncommon for these rivers to be completely dry for part of each year.

Miscellaneous

Other settlements were vacated for environmental reasons that fall under no specific heading. For example, Morristown in southeastern Idaho failed because frost came too early each year and remained late into the growing season. This led to much discouragement and the eventual failure of the community. Brigham City, Arizona, one of the Mormon settlements founded under the communal system known as the United Order, was abandoned in 1891 because of discouragement and crop failure. Georgetown, Nevada, sold its water rights to a local mining company and only existed for five years.

One of the most unusual Mormon failures was Iosepa in Skull Valley, west of Salt Lake City. In 1889, a group of Hawaiian Mormons immigrated to the "mainland" and settled in this desolate part of Utah. The inhabitants of Iosepa struggled for many years, somehow managing to survive the hardships of their new home. At its peak, over 200 persons lived in Iosepa, but the new environment proved fatal to many of the Hawaiians. Sickness was prevalent, even leprosy, and the resulting deaths soon decimated the community. In 1917 the survivors vacated Iosepa and returned to their native Hawaii.[23]

Canada and Mexico

Caldwell, in southern Alberta, was the only settlement in Canada that failed. This community slowly lost population as its inhabitants sought better land elsewhere in Canada. The LDS Church had purchased a ranch at Hillspring, ten miles away, and this enterprise attracted many persons from Caldwell.[24]

Cave Valley in Chihuahua, Mexico, was abandoned because its inhabitants gradually moved away; discouragement with communal living was a factor in its demise. Colonia Oaxaca in Sonora was vacated in 1911 when destructive floods caused by the overflow of the Bavispe River washed away most of the better soil from the farmland.

Conclusion

Fully 46 settlements failed because of "environmental factors," or 8.6 percent of the total of 537 settlements founded. But the population of these 46 defunct settlements, even at their zenith, was notably small; therefore, their loss to Mormon colonization was far less than 8.6 percent might indicate. For example, the average peak population of these 46 settlements was approximately 100 persons.[25] In other words, fewer than 5,000 persons were affected because of these settlement failures. Some of these communities consisted of only three or four families at most, and the largest ones contained no more than about 400 persons. Palmyra, Utah, had a peak population of about 412, and Colonia Oaxaca, Mexico, consisted of over 400 inhabitants before its demise. Few of the other defunct settlements had a population of more than 200.

The subclasses with settlements that had the lowest peak population are "Floods" and "Attrition." Low population could have been a factor in the demise of some of these settlements. For example, large dams were often required to control the overflow of rivers, and these impoundments could not be readily built by a community consisting of 100 persons or fewer. The settlements listed under the heading of "Attrition" also suffered from low population because it took the removal of only a few families before the community would cease to exist or become undesirable to the remaining inhabitants.

Most of the colonists did not "give up" readily. In fact, only three communities were vacated within the first year of occupancy, and some settlements lasted as long as 60 years or more before their demise. The average lifetime of these 46 settlements was 22 years, but this average is only approximate because the exact terminal date of many settlements is unknown. Nonetheless, these statistics attest to the tenacity of the Mormon venture to colonize the West and to make the "desert blossom as a rose." The significant aspect is not that 46 settlements failed, but that the marginal nature of the areas colonized by the Mormons did not lead to a much higher failure rate.

Notes

1. A notable exception is the recent work of Stephen L. Carr, *The Historical Guide to Utah Ghost Towns* (Salt Lake City: Western Epics, 1972).

2. See Leonard J. Arrington, *Great Basin Kingdom: An Economic History of the Latter-day Saints, 1830–1900* (Lincoln: University of Nebraska Press, 1958), pp. 383–84, for an explanation of the use of 1900 as a terminal date for Mormon colonization.

3. There were a few settlements in 1930 such as Grafton and Hillsdale which consisted of only twenty to thirty persons or sometimes fewer. These marginal communities have not been included in the list of defunct settlements.

4. With the exception of communities vacated because of the "Utah War" or Indian conflicts, little has been written on defunct Mormon settlements. Most of the information in this article was garnered from scattered references in Andrew Jenson's *Encyclopedic History of the Church of Jesus Christ of Latter-day Saints* (Salt Lake City: Deseret News Publishing Company, 1941) and also from various county histories, especially those compiled by the Daughters of Utah Pioneers organization. There is an article on ghost towns that lists some of the deserted Mormon settlements: "Ghost Towns of the West," in Kate B. Carter, ed., *Heart Throbs of the West*, 12 vols. (Salt Lake City: Daughters of Utah Pioneers, 1936–51), 8:133–88. The defunct settlements in southern Utah are mentioned in Herbert E. Gregory, "Population of Southern Utah," *Economic Geography* 21(1945):29–57. Settlements in the Virgin River area are described in Andrew Karl Larson, *I Was Called to Dixie—The Virgin River Basin: Unique Experiences in Mormon Pioneering* (Salt Lake City: Deseret News Publishing Company, 1961); and in Joseph Earle Spencer, "The Middle Virgin River Valley, Utah: A Study in Cultural Growth and Change" (Ph.D. diss., University of California, Berkeley, 1937). Larson's work also has some material on the Muddy River area. The best source for defunct settlements in Arizona is James H. McClintock, *Mormon Settlement in Arizona* (Phoenix: Manufacturing Stationers, Inc., 1921). This work also includes information on the Muddy River region. The outlying settlements that were vacated during the "Utah War" or because of Indian problems are presented in some detail in Milton R. Hunter, *Brigham Young the Colonizer* (Independence, Mo.: Zion's Printing and Publ. Co., 1945).

5. For an analysis of the effect of Indian conflicts on Mormon settlement, see Lynn A. Rosenvall, "Mormon Fortifications in Western North America," *Historical Archaeology in Northwestern North America,* ed. Ronald M. Getty and Knut R. Fladmark (Calgary, Alberta: The Univerisity of Calgary Archaeological Association, 1973), pp. 195–212.

6. Four of these nine settlements—Fort Limhi, Elk Mountain, Zion, and Tuba City— were eventually resettled after many years. Most of the new inhabitants were non-Mormons. They have been included in the list of defunct settlements because they ceased to be "Mormon" settlements. Fort Limhi and Elk Mountain were both resettled near the end of the nineteenth century and are now known as Lemhi and Moab. Both

were established originally as missions to the Indians. Zion is now the site for the west entrance to Zion National Park. Tuba City was subsequently occupied by Indians in the area.

7. The underlying reasons for the army coming to Utah have never been fully agreed upon. See, for example, Arrington, *Great Basin Kingdom*, pp. 170–74; and Norman F. Furniss, *The Mormon Conflict, 1850–1859* (New Haven: Yale University Press, 1960).

8. San Bernardino had a population of over 2,000 when it was vacated.

9. The site of Mormon Station is now known as Genoa.

10. These settlements were immediately occupied and controlled by non-Mormons who were starting to settle in the two areas.

11. Las Vegas was resettled in about 1900 by non-Mormons. See G. S. Dumke, "Mission to Mining Town: Early Las Vegas," *Pacific Historical Review* 22(1953):257–70.

12. For an analysis of the effect of state boundary changes on Mormon settlement patterns, see L. A. Rosenvall, "Interstate Boundaries and Settlement Patterns: The Example of Utah," B.C. *Geographical Series, Number 17* (1973), pp. 35–53.

13. See reference 20 for data on water flow extremes in the Muddy River.

14. Larson, *Virgin River Basin*, p. 150.

15. Saint Joseph is now called Logandale. Saint Thomas was subsequently vacated because man-made Lake Mead had to occupy that site.

16. See Thomas C. Romney, *The Mormon Colonies in Mexico* (Salt Lake City: Deseret News Press, 1938); and R. A. Schwartzlose, "The Cultural Geography of the Mormon Settlements in Mexico" (Master's thesis, University of California, Berkeley, 1952).

17. Leland H. Creer has written concerning the great care taken by the Mormons to gather considerable information about the Far West in general and the Great Basin in paticular before they left the Nauvoo region. See his *The Founding of an Empire: The Exploration and Colonization of Utah, 1776–1856* (Salt Lake City: Bookcraft, 1947), pp. 218–24. 218–24.

18. These exploratory expeditions are chronicled in Hunter, *Brigham Young the Colonizer*, pp. 28–54.

19. An example is Morristown, Idaho, which was founded in 1863 by dissident Mormons. The location of the settlement was poorly chosen, and they suffered many crop failures because of early and late frosts. Many of the smaller settlements—especially on

the fringes of the region—were founded by Mormons but not under ecclesiastical direction.

20. Many settlements along these rivers suffered their worst damage during the 1870s. No records were kept of the actual flow of these streams, but other sources indicate that the period of time corresponding to approximately the 1870s was a period of above-normal precipitation for the arid West. For example, the level of the Great Salt Lake, which fluctuates in relationship to the precipitation pattern of the surrounding drainage area, reached a high point in 1872 and 1873. Recent tree-ring research also indicates that this time period was characterized by above-normal precipitation in the Colorado River basin. See, for example, E. Schulman, *Dendroclimatic Changes in Semi-Arid America* (Tucson: Univeristy of Arizona Press, 1956). Stream flow records have been kept for most of these rivers since about 1900. These records verify the fact that these rivers have great extremes:

 Little Colorado River at Holbrook, Arizona:
  Average flow: 96.7 cfs (cubic feet per second)
  Maximum flow: 60,000 cfs (est.), Sept. 19, 1923
  Minimum flow: No flow at times in most years.
 Fremont River near Bicknell:
  Average flow: 90.3 cfs
  Maximum flow: 1,200 cfs, April 5, 1942 (5.8 feet above datum)
  Minimum flow: 18 cfs, June 1912
 Paria River near Cannonville:
  Average flow: Approximately 10 cfs
  Maximum flow: 5,160 cfs, Aug. 16, 1955 (9.76 feet above datum)
  Minimum flow: No flow for many days each year.
 Virgin River at Virgin, Utah:
  Average flow: 207 cfs
  Maximum flow: 13,500 cfs, March 10, 1938 (10.7 feet above datum)
  Minimum flow: 22 cfs July 10, 1920
 Muddy River near Overton:
  Average flow: 6.08 cfs
  Maximum flow: 6,500 cfs, Feb. 22, 1914 (8 to 9 feet above datum)
  Minimum flow: No flow at times in most years.

21. McClintock, *Mormon Settlement in Arizona*, pp. 141–42.

22. Larson, *Virgin River Basin*, p. 74.

23. The story of Iosepa is told in Edna Hope Gregory, "Iosepa, Kanaka Ranch," *Utah Humanities Review* 2(1948):3–9.

24. See Lawrence B. Lee, "The Mormons Come to Canada, 1887–1902," *Pacific Northwest Quarterly* 59(1968):11–12.

25. Very few population statistics are available for these defunct settlements; therefore,

other means had to be used to estimate the average peak population. The type of ecclesiastical organization in these communities was first determined, and then their population was estimated from this information. One-half of the 46 settlements had only a "branch" organization, which, using examples from other settlements, meant that their population would range from a few families (10 to 20 pesons) up to about 100 persons. The other 23 communities had "ward" organizations, which on an average had no fewer than about 100 persons, although very few were above 200. Using this method and the resulting statistics, the average peak population for the 46 settlements computes to approximately 100 persons.

Mormon Settlement in Its Global Context

Alan H. Grey

People can be so taken up with the presumed uniqueness of their experience that they fail to see its commonness. So it seems to be with the Latter-day Saints when they look back at their actual or adopted heritage. Because they do not make adequate external comparisons, they ascribe a unique status to their own customs, economy, and settlements; therefore, the ways in which they were and are one with the events of the day escape them almost entirely. Perhaps at the root of it all lies a misunderstanding of Peter's description, as it appears in the King James translation of the Bible, of the early Christians as a "peculiar people," literally a people owned by Christ.[1] Modern readers, among them the Latter-day Saints who in name and doctrine identify themselves as a renewal of early Christianity, usually and incorrectly understand the word *peculiar* to mean "different" or "strange." Accordingly, difference has long been stressed among the Mormons and has spilled far beyond doctrine into their evaluation of the material culture they created in the American West, particularly its patterns of settlement. Even without ignoring the unique locations, the imaginative use of technology, and the religious and social importance associated with these patterns, it is apparent that they have remarkable analogues elsewhere and that therefore a stress on their uniqueness gives a distorted view of their character. In order to appreciate the special and general nature of Mormon settlement, one must examine it in the wider context of an activity of which it was but a small part.

From the fifteenth century on, European people engaged in an economic, political, and personal diffusion that has left an indelible mark on geographical patterns. This complex tide crested in the nineteenth century with the migration of large numbers of people of European origin into the remote middle latitude lands. As the nineteenth century opened, North America's coastal settlements were looking westward, European settlements were old in South America and southern Africa, Australia had its small penal colony, and New Zealand was on the economic periphery of the North Atlantic countries. The century thus began with precedents established to give direction to its migrations.

Political control of this movement was diverse. In the Americas, by 1800 colonial ties to Europe had been severed or were rapidly weakening. In North America, and in the United States in particular, expansion into "empty" lands was largely governed and encouraged by the existing cores of settlement. Nineteenth-century movement into southern Africa, Australasia, and to a lesser extent Canada was generated by British interests made cautious both by recently suffered losses in North America and by the pressure of evangelical Christians' concern for indigenous populations.[2] Despite this caution, the British Empire of settlement grew modestly in response to domestic social and economic conditions. In the United States, where no such caution was practiced, the extension of settlement into an internal empire was more vigorous and unashamed.

In examining this Europeanizing of the remaining middle latitude lands, one can use a highly generalized model. Its principal components are: a cultural heritage specifically manifested in a search for power and economic advantage through geographical exploitation; an enhanced awareness of vast, apparently empty lands ready for use; the related complex of the improvement of the circulation of goods and people at a global scale; and the rapid growth of populations that accompanied what at least some people saw as the disastrous change from an agricultural-market town to an industrial-metropolitan way of life in the North Atlantic rimlands. In studying nineteenth-century settlement at the local scale, this general model is somewhat masked by the variety and richness of the individual circumstances and decisions that created local geographical patterns. Particularly, the inheritors of these patterns, their perceptions reinforced by a close association with detailed local lore, are unlikely to see what they have received in any context wider than that of their national experience. Yet even when examined at this scale, the conditions which the general model summarizes have left a mark of similarity in some very widely separated nineteenth-century settlements.[3]

In this sense, while the comparison would almost certainly surprise their Anglican and Mormon founders and present inhabitants, it is instructive to examine Christchurch, New Zealand, and Salt Lake City, Utah. Both settlements have a great deal in common. They were essentially contemporary in their founding (1851 and 1847) and had in their *raison d'être* an ideology of religious and social purpose. In situation both were, by design, at the remote margins of settlement for their period and originating populations, later becoming central places for their respective geographical regions. Each city was originally carefully laid out in a rectangular, cardinally oriented grid focused upon a proposed sacred building, later constructed; and in each, special provision was made for social amenities, particularly education.

But this similarity should not be surprising, for Christchurch (originally the Canterbury settlement) and Salt Lake City were part of a current of their times—the geographical expansion of vigorous political and economic centers. In the writings of Canterbury's leader, John Robert Godley, and in the associated founding propaganda of the Canterbury Association, the appropriateness of British imperial expansion is both unquestioned and offered as a major reason for the proposed settlement in New Zealand.[4] Godley himself earlier (1842) had been in the United States. He was somewhat critical of American ways and politics and perceived a need for diverting the inevitable emigrations from the British Isles away from America and into British colonies where the old loyalties to Crown and Church could be fostered under improved circumstances.[5] But his American experience left a mark beyond increasing his enthusiasm for British colonization. He foresaw America as a great power through its expansion and admired its vigorous Episcopalian (Anglican) Church, attributing its vigor to its virtual autonomy.[6] The Mormon leaders, Joseph Smith and Brigham Young, partook at least partially of the spirit of Manifest Destiny that seemed so natural to Americans of their day, and the founding scenes of the church they served were intimately tied into the progress of western settlement from upstate New York to the Missouri, Illinois, and Rocky Mountain frontiers. The leaders of both groups expressed strong loyalty to the political ideals of their respective core areas,[7] and while they protested when they perceived their rights under these ideals to have been abridged, they worked for redress within the political systems they were attempting to transplant in what they believed to be a purer form. Economically, the Canterbury settlement harked back unsuccessfully to the rural ideals of an earlier England, but its connections with the mother country became essentially mercantilist, although modified a little by Wakefieldian colonial theory.[8] The Mormon settlements in the Great Basin followed earlier American precedents and attempted to build a purified and independent economic kingdom that in the end failed when the penetration of the railroad made it tributary to nineteenth-century American capitalism. Through ambition, subsistent necessity, or perhaps ignorance, both groups tended to exploit rather than conserve their respective domains. Here the Mormons followed the precepts of their culture rather than of their religion.[9]

The leaders of the Canterbury and Great Basin settlements were quite aware of the opportunities offered by the empty lands to which they looked. The explorations of James Cook, fifty years of economic contact, and a decade of British settlement had made New Zealand reasonably familiar to any Englishman who took the trouble to read about it. Godley had first envisioned fostering further British settlement in Canada but was persuaded by E. G. Wakefield to direct his attention to New Zealand. For some years before their forced movement westward in 1846, the Mormon leaders had assiduously collected information on the American West from the personal and published accounts of explorers and trappers[10] and apparently had been appraised of the proper strategy for correcting the "barrenness" of the Great Basin through irrigation.[11] In both cases the founders considered their respective choices well suited to their primary aims—the recreation of an idealized English community on the one hand and the creation of a Zion in protective isolation on the other. But the necessary remoteness was at least partly mitigated by the process of settlement itself.

By the middle of the nineteenth century the globe was open to large-scale economical, two-way movement. Exploration and technical improvements had made long-distance sea and land transportation commonplace, if still arduous and risky. After just two years in Canterbury, J. R. Godley was back in England; and within months of reaching the Salt Lake Valley in 1847, Brigham Young was again with the main body of his people on the Nebraska bank of the Missouri River. Even wagon trains were not as unidirectional and noneconomical as some have suggested.[12] Neither settlement lost its physical, cultural, and political links with its originating core, but slow communications made life difficult. Godley in Canterbury complained of the remote control over very local matters exercised by the Canterbury Association in London.[13] The Utah War of 1857–58 was partly the result of misunderstanding fostered by slow communications with the national capital. But imperfect as the connections were, in both cases the return journey was possible given the money and the desire.

In their religious and social origins these two settlements were of their age. As in earlier times, the main generator of migration was a belief in greater opportunities elsewhere. However, while perceptions were most commonly of material advantages, a significant number were an expression of religion, still a major personal and social force in the nineteenth century. The economic and social turmoil accompanying the major changes in life wrought by the Industrial Revolution and the related population growth in the North Atlantic countries generated religious and quasi-religious responses as varied as the backward look of the poet Blake and the Anglican High Church movement, the forward look of millennialist Christian sects, and the various secular utopian views of which Fourierism and Marxism are among the better known. All represented some dissatisfaction with contemporary conditions of the body and spirit which at least some proposed to remedy by migration to new lands where a better social order might be constructed unmarred by local precedents. While not the most common motive for nineteenth-century migration, religion and ideology were still part of the milieu.

As with the Salt Lake oasis, the Canterbury settlement in New Zealand was founded upon explicit religious and social principles. The leader[14] of the Canterbury Association's first pilgrims was John Robert Godley, the son of an Irish, Tory, Anglican squire. Godley had been educated at Harrow School and Christ Church, Oxford, and while at the university had adhered to the new Anglo-Catholic or Tractarian Movement, which saw the need for a renewal of the English church by returning to a more autonomous primitive Catholicism. He combined this religious enthusiasm with one for colonization by British people overseas picked up on his American journey and reinforced by his personal experiences in the Irish potato famines (1845–47). Joining with Godley in initiating Canterbury was E. G. Wakefield, the colonial theorist. Something of a Benthamite, Wakefield saw in British colonization overseas benefits that in the past had been dissipated by a lack of system. With Godley, he took as his ideal the ancient Greek practice of sending out quite complete models of the originating polis for the latter's benefit.[15] Wakefield believed that recent British colonization had attracted mostly the poorer orders of society, classes ill-fitted to govern themselves. When land was made virtually free to meet their wants, the small colonial populations rapidly scattered over greater areas than they could reasonably handle, creating shortages of labor on the land itself and in the depleted prinicipal settlements. Lacking capital, and with this geographical scattering, it was almost impossible for colonies to provide the amenities of civilization. Lacking local leadership, colonies were controlled by the remote and deadening British Colonial Office. The better classes of people who could bring both capital and leadership were not inclined to move to colonies where they would not only be largely without educational and religious foundations but where they would also lose most of the privileges of self-government they enjoyed in Britain. Wakefield proposed to make colonization more balanced and systematic by charging a price for land that only the better classes of people could afford, a price just sufficient to prevent the premature movement of labor into the countryside. With this concentration, resulting from the relatively high price of land, social amenities such as churches, schools, and roads could be provided and continuing immigration subsidized. A more balanced social structure would exist from the very beginning, industrious laborers could save money to pay for land, and the colonial leaders and well-to-do would be assured of social position and adequate hired help as the colony expanded. Wakefield partially employed these ideas elsewhere in South Australia and in New Zealand,[16] but they found their fullest expression in the Canterbury settlement. Wakefield had long considered that his system could be improved by adding to it the cohesion imparted by sectarian religion and saw an instrument to suit his purposes in Godley, who had come to public attention by a forceful advocacy of systematic Irish emigration. At Wakefield's invitation, Godley met with him in November 1847, and from their discussion arose the Canterbury Association.[17]

In founding the association, Godley and Wakefield assembled an impressive list of sponsors; high prelates, noblemen, politicians, and bankers lent their prestige to an endeavor that aimed at creating an exclusively Anglican colony that would transplant a perfect model of British society, with its classes and institutions, for the relief of the mother country.[18] While all men could benefit in such a colony, the endeavor was meant to attract the dissatisfied squirearchy, "persons of refined habits and cultivated taste," rather than the more usual yeomen, small capitalists, and enterprising traders.[19]

The circumstances were ripe for such a "valuable class of men [to] be induced to join in the foundation and settlement of colonies," and many would do so if provision was made for "the appliances of civilization and the ordinances of religion."[20]

It is conceived by the promoters ... that the present time is one peculiarly fitted for bringing the plan before the public. Extraordinary changes are taking place in the political and social system of Europe; the future is dark and troubled; "men's hearts are failing them for fear;" and many persons who have been deterred hitherto by dread of change from entering into the new career afforded by colonization, will now probably be impelled into it.... More particularly ... we allude to clergymen and country gentlemen who began life, perhaps, with what was then a competency, but who now have to meet the demands produced by large and growing families, who forsee the necessity of descending to a lower station in life than they have hitherto occupied, and to whose children the crowd and pressure observable in every walk of life seem to close every reasonable chance of progress or even subsistence.[21]

In colonial life such persons would be

... living in comfort and plenty ... looking upon each additional child as an additional blessing, instead of, as now, an additional burden; enjoying a quiet and happy life in a fine climate and a beautiful country, where want is unknown; and listening from afar, with interest indeed, but without anxiety, to the din of war, to the tumult of revolutions, to the clamour of pauperism, to the struggle of classes, which wear out body and soul in our crowded and feverish Europe.[22]

Particular emphasis was to be given to the facilities and organizations for worship and education. Provision for these was to be made by allotting almost a third of the purchase price of land to the Anglican Church, which would set up a bishopric, churches, common schools, and a university college.[23] The latter was seen as being an especially necessary attraction for the class of people who could be expected to invest their means and lives in the settlement. The stability of the new settlement was to be assured by seeing to it that the original purchasers of land were Anglicans[24] of means who would "have the [privilege of the] selection of labourers to be recommended for passage; such labourers to be also exclusively *bona fide* members of the English Church."[25] By this means the Church of England would be made more vigorous by "sending forth a segment of her own body . . . which may perpetuate the preservation of her doctrine and discipline among nations yet unborn."[26] The example had been given by the American Episcopalians. The driving force in the Canterbury settlement was thus a reaction to contemporary economic and social change through a return to the stability offered by a subsistent, agrarian social order and an ancient religion. All in all the Canterbury plans, to a great extent, partook of the character of the New England idea of a "city upon a hill" which Page Smith[27] claims was responsible for the nature of much settlement in the American Middle West and which finds clear and understandable echoes in Mormon settlements.

What the Mormons did was not only in an American tradition, but was also part of a greater European restlessness which had such geographically diverse manifestations as the Canterbury and Adelaide settlements of New Zealand and South Australia and the Boer republics of South Africa. The times were changing and there was seen to be space for settlement. People who were increasingly threatened by uncomfortable changes were presumed to be amenable to going abroad and creating their society anew. To implement these aims, the founders of Canterbury and Salt Lake City needed a spiritually and physically coherent settlement removed at least to some degree from the events that generated it.

The Latter-day Saints were also seeking to avoid difficult circumstances and to build communities where a way of life could be established without interference. In their case, too, systematic settlement was considered necessary. A balance of skills (rather than social classes) was sought for each new settlement, whenever such a balance could be attained. The foundation of their settlements was also agrarian, and great attention was paid to the process of acquiring land, as was the case in Canterbury; but there were no gentlemen farmers, for land was initially allocated according to need rather than wealth. A sense of community and the requirements of irrigation kept settlers together. In

Salt Lake City and its settlements, as in Canterbury, the provision of social amenities was a major concern, although the Mormons relied upon sacrifice and cooperation rather than land sales to meet these needs, and both groups depended upon concentrated rather than diffused settlement to ensure the practicability of church, school, and social activity. Finally, in both cases provision was made for assisted immigration, although the revolving capital of the Perpetual Emigrating Fund was quite different from the provision of assisted passages from the proceeds of the sale of land at a high price. The desire to establish communities rather than simply to occupy the land at a profit accounts for these similarities, the rather divergent physical environment and social character of the two settlements for the differences.

From the number, population, and constitution of their communities, the Latter-day Saints must be considered the more successful in meeting their ideals.[28] Their reaction to the ills of the day was more theological and less socioeconomic than in Canterbury, and their religious stimulus was more powerful and encompassing, it being the generator of the social structure as well as its support. The Millennium and Zion proved in the end to be a more powerful attractive force than a fading social order interpreted through the eyes of its major beneficiaries. British converts to Mormonism, mostly from the poorer classes who were worst hit by the European economic and social changes, migrated by the thousands to the arduous endeavor of building a Zion,[29] but few English country gentry migrated to Canterbury and the life of a gentleman farmer.[30] Although essentially correct in their view of the need for systematic settlement, Godley and Wakefield misperceived the stimulus to move abroad and did not understand what Joseph Smith and Brigham Young understood very well—that leadership was much more a matter of spirit than of social class. In addition, the Mormon leaders more correctly perceived that their settlements would long be poor, subsistent, and largely self-sufficient. Canterbury's founders do not appear to have desired or appreciated that. Once on the spot, Godley recognized that in the colonial context extensive pastoral activity resulting in the export of wool was more profitable than the intensive growing of crops for what was a very small local market.[31] Within the structure devised for Canterbury there was really little economic support for a gentleman farmer. Canterbury also had such great difficulty in attracting eligible Anglicans that the religious exclusiveness of the colony was never attained, even in the first group of settlers. In 1864, 55 percent of the province was Anglican compared with a New Zealand colonial average of 42.5 percent. Two other provinces had higher percentages of their population confessing that faith.[32]

Yet, as in Salt Lake City, the religious underpinnings of Canterbury are visible in the large and costly sacred building at the focal point of Christchurch. In Canterbury, the cathedral, bishop, and clergy were as much a part of the iconography of settlement as the temple and prophet in Utah, and in both cases years and sacrifice were needed to complete the planned urban pattern.[33]

This brings up a final point. Both cities were planned and had a gridiron layout. In this they were following separate precedents,[34] but there seems to be no great significance to the gridiron apart from the fact that it is an easy and inexpensive pattern to survey and a convenient one when many people want land in haste in an orderly community. One can also find weak theological precedent in both cases if one chooses. The gridiron city is an ancient affirmation of man's desire to be properly oriented in the cosmos[35] and is not unique to the Latter-day Saints by any means. Sufficient evidence has already been presented[36] to show that this layout as expressed in Utah's towns has little but its geometry to relate it to Joseph Smith's plat of the "City of Zion" and thus has no more theological significance in Salt Lake City than in Christchurch.

So, in many elements, Salt Lake City and its associated settlements prove to be representative for the period of their founding. Certainly they are not as different in form or origin as some fondly suppose. But this is not to say that Mormon settlements were simply products of their time. That is a *post hoc* fallacy. Rather, it means that geographically specific Mormonism exists now because it was possible for its germ idea to grow in the milieu within which it arose. The revelation of a new course has little chance of influence if its necessity is unperceived, and change was an important characteristic of the nineteenth-century milieu. Without political power or economic influence, the Latter-day Saints had to move to a territory of their own or very likely suffer the fate of the Albigenses; and it helped that other millions were then doing much the same thing. In a world with dimensions and properties but newly comprehended, where it was now known that there was space for new settlements, where movement over great distances was increasingly possible, and where there were grave dissatisfactions with existing social conditions, a religion based, among other things, on a physical community and the establishment of a tangible Zion had at least a fighting chance of survival. But religious novelty aside, settlements with a purpose and a plan were not unusual in the midnineteenth century. Whatever it had that was peculiarly its own, the geographical pattern of the Latter-day Saint settlement was created of the materials of its time. Attention to this idea aids both in the understanding of the origins of Mormon settlements and in the identification of their true differences. Ultimately they *were* different within the context of nineteenth-century European expansion in the persistence within them of an almost subsistent way of life—a persistence founded in an extraordinary sense and reality of community characterized by a great measure of willingness to sacrifice for noneconomic ends of a public as well as a private kind. It is in this social and economic condition, rather than in their morphology, that the Mormon settlements showed their identity.

86

Notes

1. See 1 Peter 2:9. The meaning of being the personal property of God is shown more plainly in Titus 2:14, Exodus 19:5, and Psalm 135:4 and is supported by the *Oxford English Dictionary*.

2. As an example, there is the statement by Dandeson Coates, lay secretary of the Church Missionary Society (Anglican); quoted in W. David McIntyre and W. J. Gardner, eds., *Speeches and Documents on New Zealand History* (Oxford: Clarendon Press, 1971), pp. 4–7. Coates opposes the New Zealand Company's settlement program on the grounds that it would compromise Maori sovereignty already recognized by Britain.

3. Donald Meinig has already noted the parallel development of many cultural features in parts of Australia and the United States. See D. W. Meinig, *On the Margins of the Good Earth: The South Australian Wheat Frontier, 1869–1884* (Chicago: Association of American Geographers, 1962). A very recent recognition of parallel influences is found in Norman Bartlett *Australia and America through 200 Years: 1776–1976* (Sydney: S. U. Smith at the Fine Arts Press, 1976).

4. *Canterbury Papers*, vol. 1, Main Series (London: John W. Parker, 1850), p. 7. This set of tracts, published the year before the actual settlement was established, is a good documentary source for discerning the public intentions and philosophy of the founders of Canterbury.

5. John Robert Godley, *Letters from America*, vol. 1 (London: John Murray, 1844), pp. 36–38. In this work Godley mentioned the Mormons (then at Nauvoo); it was his feeling that they would rapidly die away. Ibid., vol. 2, p. 151.

6. C. E. Carrington, *John Robert Godley of Canterbury* (Christchurch: Whitcombe and Tombs Ltd., 1950), p. 22.

7. The view of Joseph Smith, shared by Brigham Young, is found in Doctrine and Covenants 101:77–80 and all of Section 134. Godley's views are stated in a letter to Gladstone (December 12, 1849) in James E. Fitzgerald, ed., *A Selection from the Writings and Speeches of John Robert Godley* (Christchurch: The Press Office, 1863), pp. 38, 39.

8. J. Hight, "Origin and Inception of the Canterbury Settlement," *Report of the Australian and New Zealand Association for the Advancement of Science* 23(1937):161–71.

9. On this topic see Hugh Nibley, "Brigham Young on the Environment," in H. Nibley et al., *To the Glory of God: Mormon Essays on Great Issues* (Salt Lake City: Deseret Book Company, 1974), pp. 3–29.

10. Richard Jackson, "Myth and Reality: Environmental Perception of the Mormon Pioneers," *Rocky Mountain Social Science Journal* 9(1972):35–38.

11. Ibid.

12. For example, James E. Vance, Jr., "The Oregon Trail and the Union Pacific Railroad: A Contrast in Purpose," *Annals of the Association of American Geographers* 51(1961):357–79.

13. Fitzgerald, *A Selection from the Writings and Speeches of John Robert Godley*, pp. 212–13 and 222–23.

14. Who *founded* the settlement is a debatable issue. Godley, in his letters, considered himself the prime mover. See Fitzgerald, *Writings and Speeches of John Robert Godley*, p. 246. On the other hand, E. J. Wakefield claims the credit for Edward Gibbon Wakefield. See E. J. Wakefield, ed., *The Founders of Canterbury: Being Letters from the Late Edward Gibbon Wakefield to the Late John Robert Godley and to Other Well-Known Helpers in the Foundation of the Settlement of Canterbury in New Zealand* (Christchurch: Stevens & Co., 1868), pp. vi–vii. Godley was the physical leader while Wakefield was the theoretician, although not solely so.

15. This attitude was founded in the emphasis contemporary English education placed on classical learning and shows through quite clearly in *Canterbury Papers*, vol. 1, pp. 5, 15.

16. Adelaide, South Australia, and Wellington, New Plymouth, Wanganui, Nelson, Dunedin, and Christchurch in New Zealand were Wakefield settlements. A discussion of Wakefield's ideas can be found in John C. H. Hewland, "Early Canterbury as a Wakefield Settlement" (Master's thesis, University of New Zealand, 1932). Hight, "Origin and Inception of the Canterbury Settlement," also discusses Wakefield's ideas, and almost every page of the *Canterbury Papers*, vol. 1, shows Wakefield's "fine Italian hand."

17. Carrington, *John Robert Godley of Christchurch*, pp. 49–50. See also Wakefield, *Founders of Canterbury*, pp. vi–vii, for a statement of E. G. Wakefield's interest in Godley as a "front." Wakefield had earlier been convicted of and served a prison sentence for abducting an heiress and was unable to present or promote his ideas in person in the polite society whose aid he needed.

18. *Canterbury Papers*, vol. 1, pp. 5–8. The list of sponsors shows the Archbishop of Canterbury as president at the head of a group of bishops, dukes, and other notables (pp. 3, 4). See Carrington, *John Robert Godley of Christchurch*, p. 48, for a discussion of the association's aims.

19. *Canterbury Papers*, vol. 1, p. 8.

20. Ibid., p. 6.

21. Ibid., pp. 7–8.

22. Ibid., p. 8.

23. Hight, "Origin and Inception of the Canterbury Settlement," summarizes the founders' educational plans. *Canterbury Papers,* vol. 1, has similar material scattered in the first eight pages.

24. *Canterbury Papers,* vol. 1, p. 57. This was a specific provision of the charter and was reiterated often, as in the letter of H. F. Alston, secretary of the Canterbury Association, to John Robert Godley, October 1, 1850. See *Canterbury Papers*, vol. 1, p. 236.

25. Ibid., vol. 1, p. 6.

26. Ibid., p. 8.

27. Page Smith, *As a City on a Hill: The Town in American History* (New York: Alfred A. Knopf, 1966), pp. 17–30.

28. The Canterbury Association's efforts resulted only in the establishment of Lyttleton and Christchurch. The idea did not spread because others outside the Association entered the area.

29. James B. Allen and Malcom R. Thorp, "The Mission of the Twelve to England, 1840–41: Mormon Apostles and the Working Class," *BYU Studies* 15(1975):499–526, especially pp. 499 and 500.

30. Fewer than 400 persons bought land under the scheme. See Nelville J. Northaver, "The Control of Immigration into Canterbury for the Period 1850–53" (Master's thesis, University of New Zealand, 1951), p. 50. Godley led the first settlers because no one of noble rank could be found to go with them. See also Carrington, *John Robert Godley of Christchurch*, p. 122.

31. Fitzgerald, *Writings and Speeches of John Robert Godley*, p. 214.

32. *Statistics of New Zealand for 1864, Including the Results of a Census of that Colony Taken in December of that Year Compiled from Official Records* (Auckland: W. C. Wilson for the New Zealand Government, 1866), Part 1, Table 18.

33. As in Salt Lake City, the noncommercial iconography had marked external expressions. The streets of the original plat of Christchurch are named for Anglican bishoprics, and the cathedral, started in 1864 and consecrated in 1881, dominated the center of the town until dwarfed by modern buildings on the sides of the central "square" on which it is located.

34. The Mormon settlements followed the gridiron so common to North American settlement of their and earlier times. The Canterbury settlement was laid out following in-

structions in Felix Wakefield's *Colonial Surveying* (London: John W. Parker, 1849). In this book, E. G. Wakefield's brother summarizes Col. Light's surveying experience in South Australia. The origin of Light's ideas is unknown. See also Michael Williams, "The Parkland Towns of Australia and New Zealand," *Geographical Review* 56(1966):67–89.

35. Werner Muller, *Die Heilige Stadt* (Stuttgart: W. Kohlhammer Verlag, 1961), p. 227.

36. Richard H. Jackson, "The Mormon Village: Genesis and Antecedents of the City of Zion Plan," *BYU Studies* 17 (1977):223–40. In his *The Making of Urban America: A History of City Planning in the United States* (Princeton, N.J.: Princeton University Press, 1965), pp. 466–72, John W. Reps accepts Lowry Nelson's contention that the Mormon village was derived from the City of Zion plat despite the evidence of other possible origins to be found in almost all the rest of his book.

Imprint of Agricultural Systems on the Utah Landscape

Charles S. Peterson

"Landscape," wrote Professor John B. Jackson in a recent article for the National Issues Forum, "is history made visible."[1] If landscape is history—and I like to think it can be—we may well ask what it makes visible about the Utah past. One of the observations that may be offered in reply is a statement that nineteenth century Utah produced three distinctive agricultural landscapes. Created first was the landscape of the Mormon village. Superimposed upon it but not displacing it was what may be termed a homestead landscape, upon which in turn was superimposed the landscape of dry farming. Each expressed a distinct stage in the territory's social, political, and economic growth; and remnants of each survive to enrich the history of the West.

The Mormon village landscape was introduced with the arrival of the first Latter-day Saints and was a projection of the needs and values of the Mormon people as they played upon and influenced the environment of the Great Basin. It began in Salt Lake City. The pattern is well-known—wide streets, irrigation ditches, large blocks divided into building lots which were in turn occupied by houses, flowers, trees, gardens, orchards, and barnyards. Adjacent was the "big field," surveyed and distributed in five-, ten-, or twenty-acre plots.[2] To one British traveler, the formula was simple and utilitarian:

Take half as much ground as you can irrigate, and plant it thickly with fruit-trees. Then cut it up into blocks by cutting roads through at right angles; sprinkle cottages among the blocks, and plant shade-trees along both sides of the roads. Then take the other half of your ground and spread it out in fields around your settlement, sowing to taste.[3]

In the decade after 1847, several forces combined to fix the village as the basic pattern on the early Mormon landscape. Contributing in this process was a ritualization of Mormon pioneering by which the exodus and the arrival were not merely celebrated on the twenty-fourth of July but were, in effect, relived as succeeding waves of Mormons moved to distant locations, leaving the "City of the Saints" not as refugees driven by a mob, it is true, but as children of God thrust from Eden to the hard, cruel world and charged to rebuild the garden in each desert outpost by the sweat of their brow.[4] The gold rush, too, served to strengthen the village pattern, providing as it did Mammon's counterproposal to reclaiming the desert through a restless and godless dispersion which was in every way the antithesis of the society the Saints were undertaking to establish. Indian wars also did much to fix the village landscape upon the territory. This was especially true after 1853 when the Walker War gave evidence of just how vulnerable scattered dwellings were. Even more fundamental was the fact that Church leaders came increasingly to see the village as an element important to Mormon worship. Indicative of their position on this point, as well as a general statement in support of village life, is the following from an 1882 letter to William B. Preston in Logan:

In all cases in making new settlements the Saints should be advised to gather together in villages, as has been our custom from the time of our earliest settlement in these mountain valleys. The advantages of this plan, instead of carelessly scattering out over a wide extent of country are, many and obvious to all those who have a desire to serve the Lord. By this means the people can retain their ecclesiastical organizations, have regular meetings of the quorums of the Priesthood and establish and maintain day and Sunday schools ... they can also co-operate for the good of all in financial and secular matters, in making ditches, fencing fields, building bridges and other necessary improvements. Further than this they are a mutual protection and source of strength against horse and cattle thieves, land jumpers, etc., and against hostile Indians, should there be any.[5]

Helping also to fix the village as a general element in the early Utah landscape was the fact that it was the only system of Mormon expansion that really worked. Efforts to develop heavy industry failed. The State of Deseret was rejected by Congress, and in time even the smaller confines of the Utah Territory were reduced and then reduced again. But the village succeeded, extending the sphere of Mormon influence and establishing itself as the means of Mormon growth. In this sense the vilage was fundamentally a way of building. It was the Saints, said Daniel H. Wells, a counsellor in the First Presidency, "who are to be found in the nooks and corners—in all directions—wherever there is a spring or a bit of land—building up, making the earth bring forth its products, and strengthening and enlarging the borders of Zion."[6] Finally, the village proved its worth as a means of distributing land and water. In return, the land and its appurtenant resources fixed the village and its forms upon the landscape, providing patterns that continue to reveal the ways of pioneer society.

Although these forces worked on Saints from the first, there is some evidence that it took until about 1855 for the pattern to become thoroughly established and that some early settlement proceeded without the strong control for town development that existed later. There is, for example, evidence of considerable looseness in the first beginnings in Salt Lake Valley beyond the limits of the city itself. Indeed, the village landscape never dominated Salt Lake Valley to the extent that it did remote areas. In part this was due to the fact that Salt Lake City became "a city of two peoples." Mormon and gentile, they did "not mingle anymore than oil and water"; yet their dual presence brought change in both the function and appearance that marked Salt Lake City as atypical in the Mormon landscape.[7] Working to shape the face of the landscape in another way was the Mormon feeling that Salt Lake Valley was Zion's center. In it, more than any other place, the Saints were safe. In it, Brigham Young stood guard. In it, the tendency was to regard the cradling ramparts of the Wasatch as the effective fortification. Thus secured, the Valley Saints lived on a somewhat more scattered landscape. Then too, economic activities diversified more quickly there than elsewhere, and the natural environment allowed greater laxity.[8]

Ranches also were rare on the early Utah landscape. A number of reasons may be found. In the first place, the years prior to 1868 predate America's ranching era. While trading posts and way stations had much in common with the later ranch, the Texas longhorn, the windmill, and barbed wire had not yet wrought their changes upon the landscape of the West. Furthermore, such isolated farmsteads as were located by Mormon settlers were quickly acted upon by Church leaders so as to transform them into villages. Typical in this respect were Lehi and American Fork, where isolated farms attracted the attention of Church leaders who within a year or two (about 1850) laid out towns and brought communities into being.[9] The penchant for cooperation also functioned against ranch-type settlement. Indicative of the influence of cooperation was Mapleton in Utah Valley, where a "Union" of beginning farmers from Springville joined to work one large farm, giving the area the name of "the Union Bench" long before anyone thought of "Mapleton."[10]

Totally excluded also during the first twenty years were other town forms. Mining towns did not exist, unless Patrick E. Connor's frail beginnings at Bingham and Stockton might be so credited. Nowhere was there a river town, although Callsville struggled briefly but died aborning on a parched and distant flank of the Colorado River. And nowhere was there a railroad town, although after 1869 Corinne and other railroad towns came to constitute a landscape of their own.

The village landscape was the direct result of Church planning and site selection. Particularly important in "viewing out" sites were Brigham Young, apostles with colonizing jurisdiction like Erastus Snow or E. T. Benson, and, less frequently, stake presidents.[11] Demands upon locaters were various, including the need to consider a site's relationship with other Mormon settlements. Brigham Young early established an ideal when he reported that settlements were being located every ten miles north and south from Salt Lake City. In practice, the ten-mile rule gave way; but it reflected ideas about the spacing of resources and way stations in an articulated Mormon system that were essentially sound and continued to influence site location. The committment to streets conforming with the cardinal directions together with considerations of water, land tilt, degree of fall, and frost belts functioned to give Mormon villages unity in their location and in their physical relationship with the valley environment. Line of travel was also an important consideration in site selection but usually played only a secondary role in fixing the exact location of villages. As a result, roads taking the easiest and closest way through Utah's valleys often made sharp turns as they entered towns to pick up the cardinal line of main streets. Instances in which early road developments continue to influence the landscape in this particular are Fillmore, Heber, and Logan. Accessibility of fuel, lumber, and grazing were likewise of primary importance, as on occasion were insects. Suggestive of the influence of the latter upon site location was a quip acknowledging that a new site chosen for Ogden by Brigham Young was "very productive of grain" but lamenting that it would also yield "a hundred bushels of crickets to the acre and fifty bushels of mosquitoes" as well.[12]

The landscape that emerged from Mormon planning may be viewed in terms of use. In general the impulse was inward, with functions of greatest intensity focusing on the town lot with its home, garden, and barns. The fort was a place of defense and a preliminary settlement phase from which in time houses were moved and around which memories and traditions functioned. The village itself was a sanctuary, a place of worship and a place of self-policing control. In its broader dimensions the village frequently extended the grid pattern of its streets and lots to become itself a larger four-square. Occasionally, however, geographic conditions interfered with symmetry, and villages assumed lopsided forms or, as in the case of Coalville and Centerville, strung out on a river bottom or pressed in against a mountain flank. Symmetry was sometimes a matter of development, as suggested by William Chandless's description of an elongated fort along the Weber River in 1855: "I reached the village ... a single street of cottages of some 300 yards in length, with their gardens behind, and the whole enclosed by an earthen wall, with a gateway at each end of the oblong; the wall gave rather a snug look to the place, and against Indians may be effectual."[13]

At easy access lay the fields, surveyed and assigned in the small plots of Mormon agriculture. Under one fence to begin with, but later fenced according to ownership and penetrated by landforms and irrigation ditches, the field represented one of a series of use patterns extending outward and was tied to the village by tedious but familiar coming and going that gave the entire experience something of a "Grey Elegy" effect. Beyond the fields lay the hay commons butting on the adjacent village's survey in larger, well-watered areas like Cache Valley or playing out into natural barriers in smaller, drier locales. Also nearby were the grazing commons, perhaps along river bottoms or on bench land that would later be flourishing dry farms.[14] At a greater distance, but not yet having taken on the full attributes of the open range, was the "big range" where dry stock, Church cattle, and off-season oxen and co-op herds ran. Typical were "The Barrens" on the windswept expanse of the Bear River bottoms in Cache Valley and the "big range" which extended from Kaysville toward Ogden, where overgrazing had become such a problem by 1869 that a newspaper reported that grass had wilted and died as a result of the noxious breath of sheep.[15]

The village landscape began early to lay the mark of the Mormon territoriality upon land far beyond the village confines. What may be called a "squatter's mentality" prevailed, which acknowledged that the Mormon landscape represented a valid claim to land as did mining camps or the section houses of homestead farms. If a man's home be his castle, the village represented an almost irrefutable Mormon claim. Although not one acre of farming ground was owned prior to 1868, the fields presented a claim only slightly less imposing than the village, while the commons laid a still impressive but diminished title upon the land. That the territorial claims of the village landscape were generally acknowledged and constituted a fact to be dealt with was suggested by the Utah Commission's report in 1888 that "those who hold the valleys and appropriate ... the waters ... hold Utah, and nature has fortified their position more strongly than it could be done by any Chinese Wall or artificial defense."[16]

Until 1854, Utahns pushed every effort to have the benefits of the federal land system opened to them. Relations with Captain Howard Stansbury and his surveyors were cordial and hopeful. In the early 1850s, the territorial legislature twice petitioned for congressional legislation giving quarter-section bonuses for immigration, as had been done in Oregon and New Mexico. Mormons also worked for an arrangement that would allow Mormon Battalion veterans to exercise their military options.[17] Then, as the land-claiming mechanisms of the village system matured in the mid 1850s, this changed. No longer did Mormons petition for federal land offices and surveys but actually lobbied to avoid their application.[18] Land claims might have continued to develop along the limited patterns of village extension; but in 1854, Colonel Edward Steptoe located a military grazing reserve in Rush Valley west of Salt Lake City. While the county courts had earlier been authorized to make adjacent herdground grants to various towns, land that lay at a distance had been virtually ignored. Prodded by Steptoe's action, the territorial legislature remedied the situation, making dozens of herdground grants in remote quarters during 1854 and 1855 that immediately formalized claims and use patterns. Legally, the territorial legislature was entirely without land jurisdiction; but when fortified by custom, its grants had sufficient validity to give Colonel Albert Sidney Johnston's invading army pause in 1858—although after a heated exchange Mormon claims to Rush Valley and neighboring Skull and Cedar valleys were impaired to make room for military stock.[19] Later, Governor Alfred Cumming called for the abrogation of all territorial land grants as evidence that the legislature was willing to restrict its jurisdiction to affairs legitimately within its preserve. The grants appear ultimately to have expired, but that this far reach of the Mormon landscape was translated into patented land in some cases is evidenced in Brigham Young's title to the Elkhorn Ranch in Cache Valley and the continued ownership of the Kimball Junction Ranch by the descendants of Heber C. Kimball.[20]

The village landscape also extended up the canyons of Utah's mountains. Although no one regarded the matter with the reverence felt by Gifford Pinchot when the multiple-use thrust of the conservation movement became obvious to him, Mormon patterns penetrated the higher elevations in forms closely paralleling the multiple-use now well known as the basis of forest administration.[21] Fuel, lumber, grazing, watershed, building stone, and recreation each in its way laid an extension of the village landscape into the highlands. In the first years, mountain patterns were of low intensity, leaving only a passing trace upon the landscape. In time, however, they scarred a network of barren slopes and washed gullies that according to later Forest Service reports was far more severe in Utah than in surrounding livestock states.[22]

Like erosion, the village landscape left a lasting mark. For Mormon Utah it was a three-dimensional mark of distinction and a bulwark against time and intrusion. But, the landscape's utility as an insignia of territoriality notwithstanding, Mormon country was finally penetrated by competing systems which in time left their own imprint upon the land. We turn now to the development of homestead and dry-farm landscapes in successive periods.

The quarter sections, isolated farmsteads, section line roads, and highline canals of Utah's homestead landscape were superimposed upon the earlier form in the years after 1868, giving evidence of national influences quite as certainly as did railroads and mines. The fact that the federal system did not obliterate the earlier form but rested upon the land like an overlay map is suggestive of the interplay between continuity and discontinuity in Utah's rural evolution. Important among the forces that worked to retard and soften the transition was the new landscape's dependence upon irrigation. Like the village, it could extend its forms only as far and as rapidly as water could take it. Also tending to mute the lines of change were the land tenure practices of the village system. Occupying land long held by evidence of use and extralegal recording arrangements, villagers exercised preemption and other purchase options or turned to cooperative homestead arrangements to get firm title as quickly as possible. The result was an orderly transition which, considering the amount of land alienated by the government, influenced landscapes only modestly to begin with.[23] A case in point is Brigham City, where a recent study shows land transactions working in the city's immediate environs through purchase options during the first years and later extending to less valuable and more distant irrigated lands through homesteading privileges.[24] The same trend is discernible in J. H. Martineau's excellent survey of nineteenth-century Cache Valley farmlands, some of which illustrate cooperative homesteading adjacent to towns and more conventional homesteads farther out.

Simultaneously, other forces tended to accelerate change. The Cache Valley experience would suggest that the new landscape's impact was quickened and emphasized by the proximity of the Idaho boundary. In addition, developing technology and growing capital permitted the opening of highline canals, which in some areas doubled or tripled land under irrigation in the years that coincided with the opening of federal lands.

Another accelerating influence lay in the fact that the first generation of native Utahns was now of age and in need of new land. For them the homestead represented opportunity. A common approach was to work on grading crews or freight to Montana long enough to put together an outfit as did the sons of Wellsville in northern Utah. Returning, they took wives and homesteaded lands previously held in common by Wellsville for grazing and haying. Soon their two-story log cabins and budding poplars reached out like fingers along the section lines and roads to other towns. By the early 1880s their impact upon the landscape was very much apparent. The effect was enthusiastically described by Philip S. Robinson, a British journalist who viewed

Cache Valley from the rampart of the Logan Temple, which was under construction:

The valley, reaching for twenty miles in one direction, and thirty in the other, with an average width of about ten miles, lies beneath you, level in the centre, and gradually sloping on every margin up to the mountains that bound it. Immediately underneath you, Logan spreads out its breadth of farm-land and orchard and meadow. . . . To right and left and in front, delightful villages . . . all of them miniature Logans—break the broad reaches of crop-land, with their groves of fruit-trees, and avenues of willows and carob, box-elder, poplar, and maple, while each of them seems to be stretching out an arm to the other, and all of them trying to join hands with Logan. For lines of homesteads . . . straggling away from each pretty village, and, dotting across the intervening meadows of lucerne and fields of corn, form links between them all.[25]

Elsewhere the new homesteads contributed to an already observable tendency to line or string villages. This was particularly true in Davis County, where Robinson passed "a perpetual succession of cottages coming at intervals to a head in delightful farming hamlets of the true Mormon type." String settlement also developed along the west slope of the Wellsville range, where the early farm-village scape of Deweyville and Honeyville was fleshed out by homesteads and other larger farms after the Bear River Canal Company brought water to thousands of acres in Bear River Valley (about 1890).[26]

Homesteading influenced the landscape in other ways. In the heart of the Sevier Valley, for example, the scattering influence of homesteading was so noticeable that Robinson came upon what he took to be a "deserted ranch-house" but which turned out to be the "meeting-house of the scattered ranches round." Yet in neighboring Sanpete Valley and elsewhere throughout the south, the old calculus still obtained, as evidenced in Robinson's reports of the villages themselves and references to abandoned "section houses" which stood as mute evidence of homesteads futilely undertaken or falsely marked.[27] In Grand and San Juan counties, homesteads and other federal entries showed up in the late 1870s and early 1880s, contributing to a ranching landscape at La Sal, Indian Creek, and the Carlisle and L.C. ranches. In Bluff and Moab, however, the village landscape persisted. The stockmen of Bluff particularly rejected the scattering influences of livestock raising; they maintained village-based operations until well after 1900 before gradually succumbing to the scattered ranch impulse.[28] Near Cache Valley's Hyde Park, homesteading is said to have touched the landscape in a way that could only have happened in Utah. At the lines where the quarters intersected on a rocky section northeast of town, a polygamist farmer is said to have built a four-room house with one room on each quarter section, and then to have filed on the full section in the names of himself and his three wives. True or not, the story suggests an interesting turn of land settlement.[29]

In eastern Utah, the Desert Land and Timber Culture Acts, along with various extensions of the Homestead Act, gave rise to an increasing number of entries and to landcapes that reflected a much greater response to the federal influence. Indeed, events even provoked a few land rushes, such as the Unita Basin rush of 1905 when upwards of a million acres formerly on the Ute reservation were opened to entry. In San Jaun County, homesteading combined with dry farming to create a boom in 1911, which culminated in a major post-World War I rush as veterans swelled an already considerable tide of Mormon emigrés expelled from the Mexican colonies and a growing number of people of Spanish descent. At least three influences may be observed in this landscape: the Mormon village modified by dispersed locations at Blanding and La Sal; Mexican homestead clusters in the Allen and Cottonwood drainages of the Abajo Mountains; and a strong dry-farm homestead pattern extending through the Great Sage Plain to Dove Creek and covering the Juniper slopes of the Abajo and La Sal mountains. Section-line roads, ripgut fences, one-room school houses, and isolated homesteads covered the country, elaborating the earlier village pattern.[30]

The dry-farm boom that swept the San Juan area in the decade after 1910 had its origins in northern Utah in the mid 1880s. Dry farming had not only become the great farming science of the day, it also represented the third great landscape form of rural Utah. Preoccupied with irrigation and the village settlement which it complemented, Mormons had ignored the more speculative dry farming. Nevertheless, folklore credits Brigham Young with predictions of dry-farm development at least as early as the 1860s.[31] Inadvertent experiments at Malad, and later at Levan Ridge in Juab County, led some to believe that dry-farm development was possible. Others, however, met the accounts with disbelief. David Broadhead, a central Utah farmer, is said to have been jailed for perjury when he filed a homestead claim on unwatered Levan Ridge, swearing he had raised wheat without irrigation. It would appear that he regained his freedom, for he later "proved up" on the place and fittingly named it Perjury Farm.

Investigations at Utah's Agricultural College in the late 1890s led to the establishment of the science of arid farming there and to the creation of six experimental farms spanning the length of the state by 1905. Under the leadership of John A. Widtsoe, the movement worked out the techniques of dry farming, applied capital and technology, and attracted thousands of homesteaders onto the benchlands of northern Utah, the sand hills of Davis County, and the plateau country of central and southern Utah.[32]

One such homesteader was Will Brooks. Educated at the Agricultural College in the days of Widtsoe's greatest enthusiasm, Brooks bossed a crew for the Utah Arid Farm Company, a commercial outfit which took up 8,000 acres in Juab County. The following year he moved to San Juan County, momentarily an El Dorado of the new life, where he homesteaded and took desert entry on several hundred acres, managed the Agricultural College's experimental farm there, got into the livestock business, opened a store, and taught school, all within a year or so of his arrival.[33]

Another was Pierce Hardman of Mendon in Cache Valley. Looking far and wide on Cache Valley's west side, he found no likely homestead site and finally followed his brother to Idaho's Arbon Valley in 1914 where he entered a dry-farm homestead. Building a cabin with dirt for floor and roof, he was well on his way toward proving up when he was drafted for service in World War I. On his return he purchased an additional 320 acres with a home, a windmill, and a chicken coop. Still later he acquired more land until he had well over a section. With neither tree, flower, nor garden to ease the starkness of his wheatlands, he spent the years of his early and mature manhood working early and late, tending his horses summer and winter, playing baseball summer Saturdays with the Arbon district team, entertaining fretful children through long snowed-in winters, and contemplating with pride that he had made it pay. When tractors liberated him from the winter care of horses and his children required higher education, he bought a winter home in Logan and commuted, first spring and fall, then weekly, and finally, daily during the working season. In his lifetime he had created a landscape of isolation, been part of it, and left it to erode.[34]

Taken together, the Will Brookses and the Pierce Hardmans created a new benchland and arid valley landscape after 1885. From it grew communities which were towns in little more than name—otherwise they were the scattered farmsteads of dry-land districts. Of such character were Petersboro, Alto, and Trenton in Cache Valley, and such places as the Arbon and Pocatello Valley districts along the Utah-Idaho border. A product too of the new landscape were railroad towns like Cache Junction, established about the turn of the century on the Oregon Short Line to handle the produce of Cache Valley's west side wheatlands. It was a new pattern superimposed upon the earlier two, extending beyond them and merging with farming landscapes elsewhere in the West.

What then is the larger meaning of nineteenth-century Utah's rural landscapes? At the outset, the role of the Mormon village landscape seems simple. It was the product of an effort to control an area for a singular way of life. Considering the powerful influence of "squatter's rights," or the priority of appropriation, upon the Mormon and the national mentality alike, it was an important factor in delineating the extent of Mormon territory and holding that territory against all comers. But the function of the village was not limited to territoriality. It was a sacrament upon the land—an edifice of worship. It also responded to both the resources and the contour of its environment with extraordinary affinity. Both product and creator of a powerful sense of community, its responses to economic impulses were only secondary, allowing it to enjoy a dimension for survival not often found in the exploitive landscapes of the West.

The homestead was a landscape of coming Americanization and transition. It was initially much influenced by the village. Not only did it occupy the tier of land next to the village, but it responded similarly to irrigation and other resources and was an element in what was still largely a self-sufficient life style. As such, its products as well as its influence on the landscape were general rather than specialized.

However, as responsive to the older landscapes as it was, the homestead was a statement of the larger American society and, the lightness of its touch notwithstanding, it significantly altered the direction of development in the rural scene. In time, the functions of its landscape departed the old way, looking increasingly to speculation and to commercial farming, thus accentuating its potential for larger land units and merging more with ranching and dry farming in its influences. It nevertheless remained an identifiable part of Utah's rural scene, recognizable by its imprint upon the landscape, by its dependence upon highline irrigation, and by the intermediary place it occupies in the overall landscape.

Along with later developments of the homestead, the dry farm may be said to be the landscape of union. It is commercial, specialized, truly agricultural, scientific in its origins, and an extension of landscape forms common to the wider West. As such, it bound Utah to the larger community. Unlike the early homestead landscape, it was little influenced by the village patterns. Community, whether in the narrow context of the Mormon society or the larger American scene, was only secondarily its goal. It was far-flung in patterns extending beyond the intermediate tier of the homestead landscape to valley benchlands and arid tracts scattered the length and breadth of the state. More than either of the earlier landscapes, the dry farms became what may be termed an expeditionary landscape as people first established their lonely habitations across its broad forms and then withdrew to commute.

The village, the homestead, and the dry farm are landscapes of a passing era. Sense of community, education, recreation, and economic interest have each come to spell withdrawal to urban centers. Ironically, the march from Utah's rural landscapes has occurred in reverse order to their development. The human element of the dry-farm landscape has almost disappeared, leaving dry farms a dehumanized but still very discernible mark upon the landscape. The homesteading landscape has been less fragile, but has still been subject to mechanization and urban influences. The village landscape too is hard hit, but echoes of its former community retard the exodus. Remnants of a bygone era, Utah's early landscapes are still the insignia of cultural diversity and change. They are a point of reference and contribute to a lingering sense of territoriality, but as distinguishing marks they give impulses of diminishing strength as time and progress work upon them.

104

Notes

1. John B. Jackson, "The Landscape of States," *Courses by Newspaper: American Issues Forum*, no. 6.

2. Mormon settlement is treated in many works. Useful among these are Milton R. Hunter, *Brigham Young the Colonizer* (Salt Lake City; Deseret News Press, 1940); G. Lowry Nelson, *The Mormon Village* (Salt Lake City: Univerisity of Utah Press, 1952); Nels Anderson, *Desert Saints: The Mormon Frontier in Utah* (Chicago: University of Chicago Press, 1942); Leonard J. Arrington, *Great Basin Kingdom: Economic History of the Latter-Day-Saints 1830–1900* (Cambridge: Harvard University Press, 1958); and Andrew Love Neff, *History of Utah 1847–1869* (Salt Lake City: Deseret News Press, 1949).

3. Philip S. Robinson, *Sinners and Saints* (Boston: Roberts Brothers, 1883), p. 146.

4. Most of the sources cited in reference 2 apply here as well.

5. James R. Clark, comp., *Messages of the First Presidency* 5 vols. (Salt Lake City: Bookcraft, 1965), 2:350–51.

6. *Journal of Discourses*, 26 vols. (London: Latter-day Saints' Book Depot, 1855–86), 19:370.

7. Robinson, *Sinners and Saints*, p. 71. In a recent study, Wayne Wahlquist convincingly argues that the village pattern was far less dominant on the Wasatch Front than elsewhere. See "Settlement Processes in the Mormon Core Area, 1847–1890" (Ph.D. diss., University of Nebraska, 1974).

8. For an argument that the tradition of desert scarcity has been overworked for pioneer Salt Lake Valley, see Richard H. Jackson, "Righteousness and Environmental Change: The Mormons and the Environment," *Charles Redd Monographs in Western History*, no. 5, ed. Thomas G. Alexander (Provo: Brigham Young University Press, 1975), pp. 21–42.

9. Nelson, *The Mormon Village*, p. 179; and Hamilton Gardner, *History of Lehi Including a Bioraphical Section* (Salt Lake City: Deseret News Press, 1913), pp. 10–28.

10. Ralph K. Harmer, "A History of Mapleton, Utah to 1945" (M.S. thesis, Utah State Univerity, 1975).

11. For the role of Church leaders in site selection, see Charles S. Peterson, *Take Up Your Mission: Mormon Colonization along the Little Colorado River, 1870–1900* (Tucson: University of Arizona Press, 1973), pp. 15–38.

12. Journal History of The Church of Jesus Christ of Latter-day Saints, LDS Archives, Salt Lake City, September 1–3, 1849.

13. William Chandless, *A Visit to Salt Lake* (London: Smith, Elder, and Co., 1857), p. 230.

14. Surveys made in Cache Valley during the 1860s by J. H. Martineau show herd grounds and haying commons as well as villages in effective relationship to each other. These are part of the county record and are at the Cache County Court House. See also Nelson, *The Mormon Village*, pp. 138 and 139.

15. Glen M. Leonard, "A History of Farmington, Utah, 1890" (M.A. thesis, University of Utah, 1966), p. 121; A. J. Simmonds, *On the Big Range, A Centennial History of Cornish and Trenton, Cache County, Utah, 1870–1970* (Logan: Utah State University Press, 1970), pp. 15–21; and *Salt Lake Daily Telegraph*, May 15, 1869. (The *Telegraph* had been moved to Ogden to cover the continental railroad's development.)

16. *Report of the Utah Commission to the Secretary of the Interior*, September 24, 1888 (Washington, D.C., 1888), p. 16.

17. Dale L. Morgan, "The State of Deseret," *Utah Historical Quarterly* 8(1940):80–81; and U.S. Congress, Senate, *Congressional Globe*, 33d Cong., 1st Sess., p. 1092.

18. Brigham Young to William H. Hooper, March 8, April 12, and May 24, 1860, quoted in Howard Lamar, *The Far Southwest, 1846–1912: A Territorial History* (Cambridge: Harvard University Press, 1966), p. 356.

19. Reference is made to the land grants by Hosea Stout, *On the Mormon Frontier: The Diary of Hosea Stout 1844–1861*, ed. Juanita Brooks, vol. 2 (Salt Lake City: University of Utah Press, 1964), entries for December and January 1854–55, 1855–56, 1856–57; see also Charles S. Peterson, "A Historical Analysis of Territorial Government in Utah Under Alfred Cumming, 1857–1862" (M.A. thesis, Brigham Young University, 1958), pp. 172–75.

20. John Hansen, "The History of College and Young Wards, Cache County Utah" (Master's thesis, Utah State University, 1968), pp. 8–10.

21. Gifford Pinchot, *Breaking New Ground* (New York: Harcourt, 1947) pp. 322–23.

22. For example, see Diary of Albert F. Potter's Wasatch Survey, July 1, November 22, 1902; and C. E. Rackford, Memorandum for the Forester, September 12, 1921, Region IV Papers, Record Group 95, National Archives.

23. George W. Rollins, "Land Policies of the United States as Applied to Utah to 1910," *Utah Historical Quarterly* 20(July 1952): 239–51; and Lawrence B. Lee, "Homesteading in Zion," ibid., 28(January 1960): 29–38.

24. Wahlquist, "Mormon Core," pp. 214–23.

25. Robinson, *Sinners and Saints*, p. 141.

26. This is treated in newspaper accounts of the era. See also Charles H. Brough, *Irrigation in Utah* (Baltimore: The Johns Hopkins Press, 1898).

27. Robinson, *Sinners and Saints*, p. 183.

28. Charles S. Peterson, *Look to the Mountains: Southeastern Utah and the La Sal National Forest* (Provo: Brigham Young University Press, 1975), pp. 50–57.

29. From an interview with Spencer Daines of North Logan, November 15, 1975. I have been unable to verify this story among other natives of Hyde Park.

30. Peterson, *Look to the Mountains*, pp. 156–65.

31. Lars Frederickson, *History of Weston, Idaho,* ed. A. J. Simmonds (Logan: Utah State University Press, 1972), p. 32; J. A. Leishman, "Dry Land Farming and Farmers," *Deseret Farmer* (December 8, 1904), p. 1; and Norah E. Zink, "Dry Farming Adjustments in Utah" (Ph.D. diss., University of Chicago, 1937), p. 9.

32. Paragraphs on John A. Widtsoe's role in dry farming depend on my earlier article, "The Americanization of Utah's Agriculture," *Utah Historical Quarterly* 42(Spring 1974): 114–15; and Grant Cannon, "Dry Farming . . .," *The Farm Quarterly* (Winter 1954), p. 43.

33. Interviews with Mr. Hardman, January and February 1972.

34. Juanita Brooks, *Uncle Will Tells His Own Story* (Salt Lake City: Taggert and Co., 1970), pp. 95–97, 103–18.

Population Growth in the Mormon Core Area: 1847–90

Wayne L. Wahlquist

Introduction

The western migration of Mormons to the Great Basin was part of the mass migration of Americans to their western frontiers. An era of "manifest destiny" and pioneering in the American West had caught the imagination of hundreds of thousands of people from Europe as well as the eastern United States. Through the decades 1850 to 1890, there was a virtual population explosion in every western territory. Seen in its proper perspective, the emigration of Mormons from Europe and their trek to the Salt Lake Valley was but a small segment of the mass emigration of Europeans to the New World, and but a single episode illustrating the lure of the frontier for hundreds of thousands of them.

Nevertheless, the growth of the Mormon population in the Salt Lake Valley was phenomenal. With the exception of gold, nothing attracted such an ethnic variety of peoples in such large numbers to the arid West as this new millennial religion, with its doctrine of "the gathering." Thousands of Mormon converts in the eastern states and Europe anxiously awaited the opportunity to migrate to the new "Zion" in the Rocky Mountains.

Greater insights into the settlement process and the contribution to western settlement of these religious migrants can be gained by an analysis of the nature of the population. One must first ask, how many Mormons migrated to the Salt Lake Valley, and what was their rate of natural increase? Secondly, what were the age and sex characteristics of that population? And thirdly, what were their ethnic origins?

Estimated Number of Immigrants to Salt Lake Valley

The actual number of Mormons migrating to the Salt Lake Valley is unknown. The arrival of Church-organized emigration companies was usually recorded by the Church historian and/or noted in the local newspaper. Some Mormons, however, came with independent companies, with freight companies, or as part of a California- or Oregon-bound wagon train. They were not recorded by the Church historian nor noted in the newspaper. Andrew Jensen, Church historian at the turn of the century, estimated that 80,000 pioneers crossed the plains prior to the completion of the railroad in 1869. Of these, approximately 6,000 died enroute.[1] Jensen's estimate has been quoted over and over again until it is firmly rooted in Mormon folklore, but it is unquestionably too high. The total population of the territory of Utah in 1870 was only 86,786 according to the U.S. census, just slightly more than the number of pioneers according to the Jensen estimate. Furthermore, the U.S. census included approximately 15,000 non-Mormons as well as several thousand Latter-day Saints who had arrived via the railroad in 1869 and 1870.[2] If 74,000 Mormons arrived in Utah prior to the completion of the railroad in 1869, sterility must have been a major problem if the total population of the territory had only increased to 86,000 by 1870. Deaths and migration out of the territory were not sufficient to account for such a slow rate of growth.

Difficulty of Obtaining Accurate Population Estimates

Accurate estimates of early Mormon population are hard to find. Mormons themselves expressed great optimism in their ability to attract large numbers of converts to their new "Zion" and the ability of the newly founded communities to assimilate and support them. The "Fourth General Epistle" (Dec. 11, 1850) even stated that they expected to double their population annually:

The crops have been abundant in all the settlements of Deseret, this season; and we have made every exertion to have them secured for the benefit of all; and although from the best information obtained we have reason to expect that our population will be strengthened nearly if not quite 15,000 this season. Yet we are confident if all will be prudent there will be seed grain and bread sufficient to sustain the whole until another harvest.

Yes, the estimated population of 15,000 inhabitants in Deseret the past year, having raised grain sufficient to sustain the 30,000 for the coming year inspires us confidently to believe that the 30,000 the coming year can raise sufficient for 60,000 the succeeding year and to this object and end our energies will be exerted to double our population annually by the assistance of the perpetual immigration poor fund and otherwise provide for the sustenance of that population.[3]

The present author doubts that even Mormon leaders honestly expected to achieve that kind of expansion, but it must have sounded exhilarating to Mormons camped along the Missouri River or waiting in Europe for an opportunity to come. These statements no doubt contributed to inflated estimates of the numbers actually arriving.

Furthermore, Utah was anxious for statehood in order to gain autonomy in state government. Mormons tended to exaggerate their numbers in order to strengthen their case.

Governor Brigham Young included the following statement in his address to the territorial legislature in December 1856:

In accordance with acts of the legislative assembly, a Constitution was formed and adopted, the census taken, and delegates chosen to present our application to congress for admission into the Union as a sovereign and independent state. Recent advices from our delegates show that our application has not been presented, owing to intolerance evinced by the predominant party in the House of Representatives.

The enumeration of the inhabitants showed a population of near 77,000 in this territory, and it is presumed that the addition to our numbers, since that was taken, would amount to about twenty thousand. This gives an aggregate equal to or exceeding the ratio of representation for congressmen, removing every objection, if any were made, to our admission, on the score of insufficient population.[4]

Critics accused them of counting livestock and unborn babies in their 1856 territorial census.[5] More likely, they were counting friends and relatives in the eastern states and in Europe who were planning to migrate in the near future. Whatever they were counting, it was not accurate. The territorial census of 1856 (76,335) was highly inflated.

On the other hand, anti-Mormon sentiment was high among the gentile residents of the territory, who were vehemently opposed to statehood and, therefore, wished to minimize the number of people living in the territory. Federal appointments were almost totally in the hands of the gentiles after 1857, which meant that those responsible for the census may have been inclined to turn in low returns. The problem was summed up well by Richard F. Burton:

110

I found it impossible to arrive at a true estimate of the population.... The Mormons, desiring to show the 100,000 persons which entitle them to claim admission as a state into the Union, are naturally disposed to exaggerate their numbers.... On the other hand, the anti-Mormons are as naturally inclined to underestimate: Moreover, as the "census marshals" received but three halfpence per head, they are by no means disposed to pay a shilling for the trouble of ransacking every ranch and canyon where the people repair for grazing and other purposes. The nearest approach to the truth will probably be met by assuming the two opposite extremes, and by "splitting the difference."

In 1849, Mr. Kelley estimated the Mormons to be "about 5,000 inhabitants in the town and 7,000 more in the settlement." In 1850 the seventh official census of the United States numbered the inhabitants of Utah Territory at 11,354 free plus 26 slaves—11,380 souls. In 1853 the Saints were reckoned at 25,000 by the gentiles, and 30,000 to 35,000 by Mr. O. Pratt, in the "Seer." In 1854, Dr. S. W. Richards estimated the number at "probably from 40,000 to 50,000" in the United States, and in Great Britain at 29,797. In 1856, the Mormon census gave 76,335 souls.... In 1858 the Peace Commissioners sent to Utah Territory reported that the Saints did not exceed 40,000 to 50,000 souls, half of them foreigners.... In 1859 M. Remy made the number of Saints in Utah Territory, not including Nevada, 80,000 souls, and the total in the world 186,000. The last official census, in 1860, was taken under peculiar disadvantages. General Burr, of the firm of Hockaday and Burr, was appointed to that duty by Mr. Dotson, the anti-Mormon federal marshal. But as the choice excited loud murmurs, the task was committed to a clerk in the general's store, and deputies for the rest of the Territory were similarly chosen. The consequence is that the gentile marshal's census of 1860 offers a number of 40,266 free plus 29 slaves—a total of 40,295 souls; while the Mormons assert their Territory to contain from 90,000 to 100,000 and the world to hold from 300,000 to 400,000 Saints.[6]

Estimates of population run consistently higher than the actual enumeration of people by both the federal census and the territorial census, with the exception of the 1856 territorial census. Church records of membership are even more conservative. Table 1 shows these enumerations for the years that they are available. The returns of the territorial census of 1851, which was taken in June before new immigrants began arriving, must have missed a number of families, since the totals were lower than those of the federal census of 1850.

Evidently there were either a considerable number of Mormons who did not have their names on the Church rolls in 1852 or 1853, or gentiles made up a larger proportion of the population than is usually thought. Figures from the Bishops Reports of 1852 and 1853 are definitely low. The total population could hardly have been less than 24,000 in 1853 and may have been as high a 35,000; yet the Bishops Report shows only 18,200 Mormons. If that report was complete, a quarter or more of the population was non-Mormon, which seems most unlikely in 1853. Some non-Mormons had been present from the time of the first settlement, and their numbers were augmented by California gold seekers who decided to stay in Utah. According to one estimate, 3,000 stayed in Utah during the winter of 1849-50; but, no doubt, most of them moved on to California the following summer.[7] They probably constituted a small minority in 1853. However, their numbers increased rapidly with the development of mining in the '60s and '70s. Gentiles were thought to number about 15,000 in 1870 and nearly 37,000 by 1880, when they comprised aproximately one-third of the population.[8]

Growth Rates

Before proceeding to further analysis of population estimates, it would be well to establish reasonable estimates of growth rates.

In contrast to other frontier areas in the western United States, the female population in Utah was approximately equal to and sometimes exceeded the male population. The statistical atlas of the U. S. Bureau of the Census for 1900 shows 3 counties in Utah, 1 in South Dakota, 1 in Kansas, and 2 in Texas as the only counties west of the Mississippi to have more females than males. Mormonism encouraged large families, which, combined with polygamous marriages, resulted in a very high birth rate. The actual birth rate is unknown, but it must have approached and perhaps exceeded 50 per 1,000. The 1880 U.S. Census of Vital Statistics indicates that Utah had the second highest birth rate in the nation, at 41.2 per thousand population—exceeded only by Arkansas with 42.7 per thousand. Utah had the highest rate of births per 1,000 women between 15 and 49 years of age—198.9. Arkansas was second with 190. These compare with New Hampshire's 71.6 and New York's 93.9. For 1880 the Utah death rate was 15.09 per 1,000 compared wih 12.77 in 1870 and 12.54 in 1860. Dr. John S. Billings, U. S. Army surgeon and author of the introduction to the Vital Statistics

112

volume of 1880 U.S. Census, stated that the rising death rate represented a more accurate enumeration of deaths in 1880 rather than an
actual increase in the death rates. However, by comparing the census
enumeration with the number of deaths recorded by physicians in two
states, Massachusetts and New Jersey, he found the census enumeration
still deficient. Projecting this deficiency to the national level, Dr. Billings believed that the actual death rate for the nation was about 18
per 1,000 population.[9] If the same ratio between actual and census
enumeration death rates held true for Utah, Utah's death rate was between 19 and 20 per 1,000.

TABLE I
CENSUS OF POPULATION IN THE
TERRITORY OF UTAH

Year	U.S. Federal Census	Utah Territorial Census	Church Membership Record
1848			1,671[a]
1850	11,380		
1851 (June)		11,354[b]	
1852			11,847[c]
1853			18,206[d]
1856		76,335[d]	
1860	40,786		
1870	86,786		
1872		105,229[e]	
1880	143,963		105,229[f]
1890	207,905		141,602[f]

[a]"Journal History of Brigham Young" 1848, p. 15, Salt Lake City, LDS Church Archives.

[b]Utah Census File, LDS Church Archives.

[c]Annual Bishops Report (available only for the year 1852 and 1853), "LDS Journal History" Dec. 31, 1852, pp. 1–3; Salt Lake City, LDS Church Archives, and *Deseret News*,
Oct. 15, 1853. The Journal History, Oct. 6, 1855, includes Bishops Reports for all Utah
settlements except Salt Lake City.

[d]"LDS Journal History," March 1, 1860, pp. 2–3; also Burton, *The City of the Saints*, p.
294.

[e]Utah Census File, LDS Church Archives.

[f]Annual Statistical Report (begins in 1878), LDS Archives.

At the same time, Dr. Billings thought that the number of births enumerated by the Tenth Census was also deficient by 15 percent, the actual national birth rate being about 36 per 1,000.[10] If the same ratio of error held true for Utah, Utah's true birth rate in 1880 was approximately 47.4 per 1,000 rather than 41.2 as recorded in the census. As late as 1915, the Mormon birth rate was 40.2 per 1,000 and had only dropped to 39.4 in 1954 and 27.2 in 1965 according to Church records.[11] The birth rate of Mormons has always been high. The number of polygamous marriages reached its lowest ebb in 1880.[12] Thus the number of polygamous marriages was lower at the time of the 1880 census than it had been previously; consequently, the birth rate for 1880 may not be representative of previous decades. The Mormon birth rate for the 1850–1890 period probably fluctuated between 47 and 50 per 1,000 population. During the same period, the death rate probably fluctuated between 17 and 20 per 1,000 even though the census figures for both rates are lower. This would result in an annual increase of births over deaths of 28 to 30 per 1,000, or 2.8 to 3.0 percent—a growth rate which is comparable to that of many underdeveloped countries today.

Population Estimates for the Years 1847–1870

In the opinion of this author, the most accurate estimates of total yearly population for the territory of Utah can be obtained by calculating population projections utilizing the aforementioned growth rates and the recorded immigration. Andrew Jensen compiled (primarily from the *Millennial Star*) manuscript histories of the incoming immigration companies that usually included the number, if not the names, of those persons arriving in each company. Jensen's manuscript histories provided the basis for a report prepared by the Church Historian's Office in 1971 which indicates each immigration company arriving in the Salt Lake Valley prior to the coming of the railroad. It is the most accurate record yet compiled. As mentioned earlier, a number of immigrants, both Mormon and gentile, arrived independently of these organized companies. There is no way to estimate accurately the numbers arriving independently, but it is the opinion of the writer that that number was relatively small. Furthermore, not all Mormons arriving in Utah remained there. Some were lured on to the goldfields of California, some became disillusioned and returned to the States,

114

and some colonized areas outside of Utah; thus the number of those uncounted immigrants arriving in the valley would be partially offset by the number who were leaving. Consequently, a net increase of 10 percent was added to the number of recorded immigrants for each year. Using that total and calculating an annual growth rate of 2.9 percent, Table 2 was prepared, indicating the total population each year from 1847 to 1870. The estimates consistently exceed the U. S. census enumerations, but the differences are slight. For 1850, Table 2 is .3 percent higher than the U.S. census, 15 percent higher in 1860, and 12 percent higher in 1870.

Since census enumerations are traditionally lower than the actual population and the calculated population consistently remains slightly above the actual census count, Table 2 represents a fairly accurate yearly enumeration of Utah's population.

It appears that the gentile estimates of the population—25,000 in 1853, and 40,000 to 50,000 in 1858—were fairly accurate, while the Mormon estimates—30,000 to 35,000 in 1853, and 90,000 to 100,000 in 1860—were grossly exaggerated, particularly the latter. The U.S. census of population in 1860, which indicated a population of 40,786, was in reality fairly accurate, although it received much criticism in Utah at the time and was thought to be much too low by Burton and later by Bancroft.

Proportion of Population Living in the Wasatch Front

Although colonization of outlying regions began soon after the arrival in Salt Lake City, the majority of Utah's population remained in the Wasatch Front area. The five counties along the Wasatch Front—Utah, Salt Lake, Davis, Weber, and Box Elder—accounted for 91.05 percent of the territorial population in 1850, 68.86 percent in 1860, 54.98 percent in 1870, 51.64 percent in 1880, and 57.74 percent in 1890.[13]

The declining percentage of people along the Wasatch Front between 1850 and 1880 indicates that colonization beyond the Front was heavy, since the actual population of Wasatch Front counties increased from 10,316 to 74,344 during that same period. However, by 1890 urbanization had reversed that declining trend; consequently, the percentage of population along the Front compared to the total population of the territory began to increase as migration to the frontier

TABLE 2
ESTIMATED POPULATION OF
UTAH TERRITORY, 1847–1870

Year	Recorded[a] Immigration	Recorded[b] Immigration Plus 10 Percent	Total Population[b] At End of Year Based on 2.9 Percent Growth
1847	1,637	1,801	1,853
1848	2,408	2,649	4,633
1849	2,004	2,204	7,035
1850	3,692	4,061	11,418
1851	3,000	3,300	15,145
1852	4,871	5,358	21,098
1853	2,798	3,078	24,877
1854	3,086	3,395	29,064
1855	2,017	2,219	32,190
1856	3,081	3,395	36,611
1857	1,414	1,555	39,273
1858	179	197	40,615
1859	1,441	1,585	43,424
1860	2,087	2,296	47,046
1861	3,641	4,005	52,531
1862	5,031	5,534	59,749
1863	3,625	3,987	65,584
1864	2,474	2,721	70,286
1865	300	330	72,664
1866	3,126	3,439	78,310
1867	500	550	81,147
1868	3,958	4,354	87,981
1869	2,321[c]	2,785	93,398
1870	910[c]	1,091	97,229

[a]"Manuscript Histories of Pioneer Companies," vol. I, Introduction, LDS Church Archives, Salt Lake City.

[b]Calculation by the author.

[c]After the completion of the railroad, accurate records were not kept. This figure represents the total of European immigrants leaving Liverpool. They were thus increased by 20 percent.

declined and many people moved from the frontier to the more developed areas nearer to Salt Lake City to seek better employment (see Figure 1).

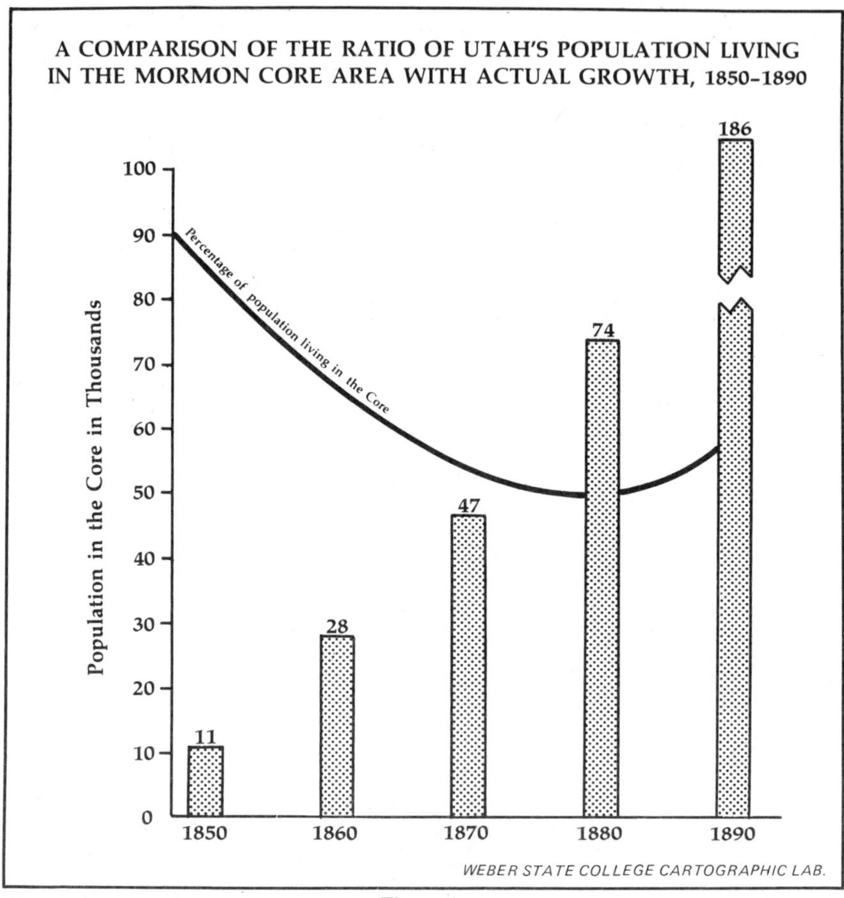

Figure 1

A COMPARISON OF THE RATIO OF UTAH'S POPULATION LIVING IN THE
MORMOM CORE AREA WITH ACTUAL GROWTH, 1850–1890

Characteristics of the Population

Age and Sex Structure

To obtain an accurate analysis of population characteristics along
the Wasatch Front, twelve settlements (see Figure 2) were selected for
detailed study. They include several small villages as well as larger

Corinne
Brigham City
Willard
Wasatch
Ogden River
Great
Ogden
Weber River
Salt
Farmington
Bountiful
Lake
Salt Lake City
Mountains
Oquirrh
Jordan River
Alpine
Lehi
American Fork
Utah
Provo
Lake
N
Payson
10   0   10
miles
WEBER STATE COLLEGE CARTOGRAPHIC LAB.

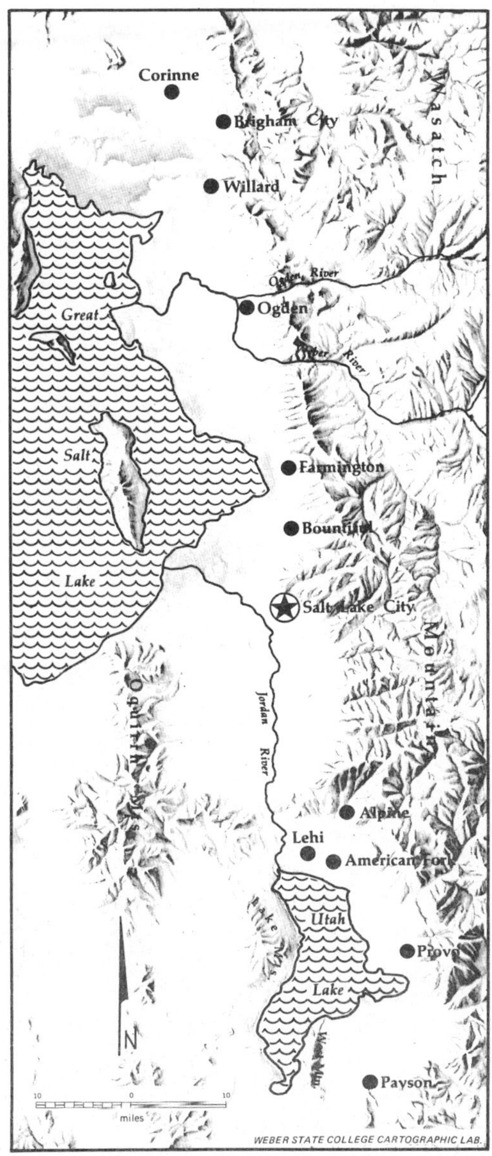

Figure 2

118

towns and were selected at frequent intervals along the Front in order
to represent the entire Core area. The published compendium volumes
of the U.S. census do not give a breakdown of the age, sex, occupation, and nativity of the population by town. Therefore, in order to
tabulate the above information by town, it was necessary to examine
carefully the manuscript population census schedules, which list each
resident of the territory by name along with his race, sex, age, occupation, and place of birth. The 1870 census year was chosen because it
marked the approximate midpoint between the first settlement in 1847
and statehood in 1896. In addition, 1870 marked the end of the pre-
railroad era. The railroad had been completed in 1869, but had not
had time to greatly effect the basic population structure of individual
settlements except those towns or cities where railroad construction
workers comprised a significant proportion of the population. Ogden
and Willard had small minorities of Chinese laborers employed by the
railroad company, while Corinne, the epitome of a railroad town, had
only come into existence the year before and was completely depen-
dent upon the railroad. Most of the settlements along the Wasatch
Front had not experienced much impact from the railroad by 1870 in-
sofar as their social structure was concerned. These settlements had
been in existence for nearly twenty years, and their internal social and
economic structure had had sufficient time to solidify.

Table 3 provides a synopsis of the age and sex structure of these relatively mature communities. Corinne in the north was the only new
community as well as the only non-Mormon settlement, since it was
founded with the completion of the railroad the previous year. With
the exception of Corinne, the most striking characteristic of the settlements shown in Table 3 is their uniformity. The variation in the sex
ratio was extremely slight except for Corinne. Willard had the highest
percentage of males with 53.4 percent (this included 31 Chinese railroad construction workers), and the lowest was Bountiful with 49.8
percent. The percentage of children under 15 years of age also varied
only slightly throughout the eleven Mormon settlements. The highest
was American Fork wih 52.3 percent and the lowest was Willard (44.7
percent), which was affected slightly by its small minority of single
railroad workers. The uniformity in age and sex structure throughout
the core settlements is indicative of the importance Mormons placed

on family life and the stabilized social structure of the population in each settlement in 1870.

TABLE 3

**SUMMARY OF AGE, AND SEX CHARACTERISTICS
OF THE POPULATION OF SELECTED
SETTLEMENTS ALONG THE WASATCH FRONT
COMPILED FROM THE 1870 MANUSCRIPT
U.S. POPULATION CENSUS SCHEDULES**

Town	Total	Male	%	Female	%	Under 15 yrs of age	%
Alpine City	208	107	51.4	101	48.6	106	51.0
American Fork	1,115	556	9.9	559	50.1	583	52.3
Bountiful	1,516	755	49.8	761	50.2	748	49.3
Brigham City	1,312	656	50.0	656	50.0	639	48.7
Corinne	777	588	65.4	269	34.6	175	22.5
Farmington	896	459	51.2	437	48.8	434	48.5
Lehi	1,058	522	49.3	536	50.7	528	49.9
Ogden	3,200	1,650	51.6	1,550	48.4	1,610	50.3
Payson	1,436	721	50.2	715	49.8	664	46.2
Provo City	2,384	1,207	50.6	1,177	49.4	1,182	49.6
Salt Lake City	12,910	6,950	50.3	6,860	49.7	6,420	46.5
Willard	552	295	53.4	257	46.6	247	44.7
Mean %			51.9		48.1		46.6

Age Structure

Not only was the percentage of children under 15 remarkably uniform throughout the core, it was also surprisingly high. Two settlements—Alpine City and American Fork—had slightly over half of their population in this age group, and the other settlements approached 50 percent. The one major exception to the rule was the gentile city of Corinne, where only 22.5 percent of the population fell into this category. The predominance of males and the low percentage of children clearly distinguishes Corinne from the Mormon settlements. The mean percentage of persons under 15 years of age for all the settlements was 48.1 percent—a higher ratio than that of most developing countries today.[14] In earlier years the percentage of children was even higher.

The 1855 Bishops Report included the number of children under 8 years of age for 32 Utah communities (excluding Salt Lake City). The mean ratio of children under 8 to the total population was 32 percent and varied from a high of 46 percent in Box Elder to a low of 20 percent in Manti. Only 11 of the 32 settlements had less than 30 percent of their population under 8 years of age.

The high percentage of children in these early Mormon communities combined with a fairly high proportion of women must have placed a heavy burden on the working population. Of course, in a rural setting, children were counted as hands as well as mouths and no doubt contributed a significant amount of labor to the family livelihood. Virtually every family had a vegetable garden that accounted for a substantial portion of its diet. Still, in many of these settlements less than half of the working population was engaged in agriculture. For non-agriculture families, such a high proportion of children must have strained their ability to provide adequate food, clothing, and shelter.

The high proportion of children also meant that a high growth rate would be maintained as these children reached the childbearing age. There would be a continual need for expanding employment opportunities in the cities and/or expanding irrigation facilities to bring more land under cultivation in order to accommodate the growing number of young native farmers as well as the continual influx of immigrants. It also meant that there was a great need for schools.

In order to examine the nature of the population in more detail, age-sex pyramids were constructed for three communities—Brigham City in the north, Kaysville near the center, and Springville in the south of the Wasatch Front area. Comparable pyramids were constructed for the years 1860 and 1880 in order to identify changing trends (see Figures 3, 4 and 5).

The true pyramid shape of the age-sex diagrams with a staircase effect from a broad base to a narrow top is indicative of a young population. Brigham City in 1860 had a particularly high proportion of children. The Bishops Report of 1855 indicated that 46 percent of the population was under eight years of age. The proportion of children in 1860 was declining but remained high. Approximately one quarter of the population was under five and 42 percent under ten years of age. At the same time only about 7 percent of the population was over for-

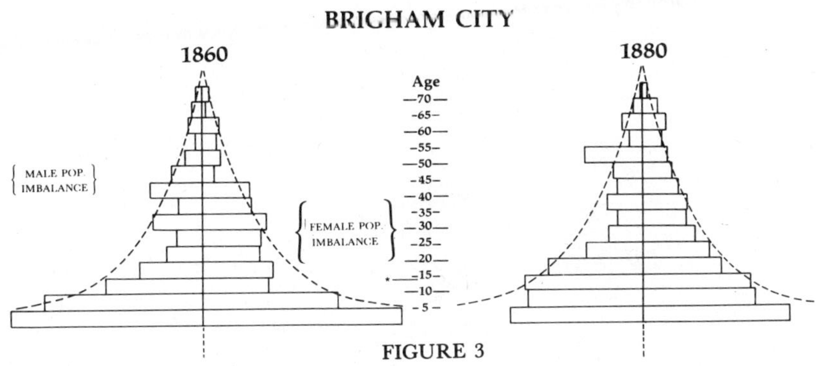

FIGURE 3

PERCENT OF CHANGE IN AGE/SEX
DISTRIBUTION
1860–1880

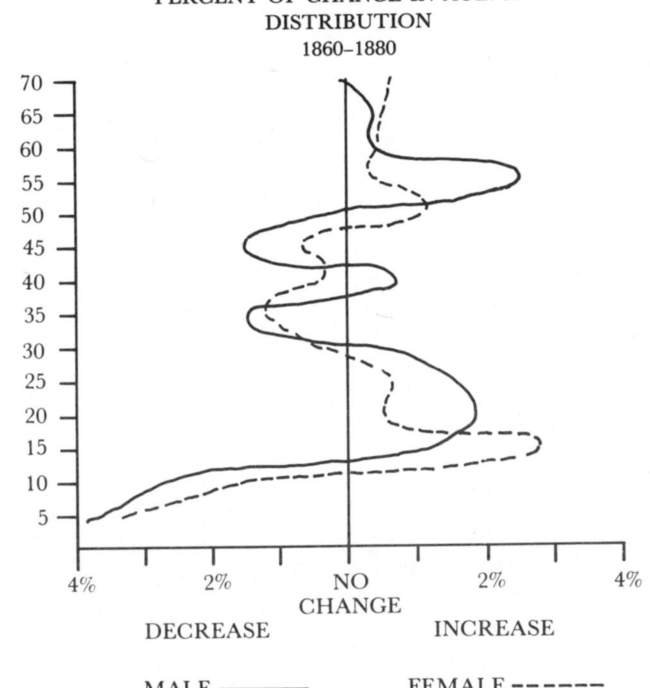

FIGURE 3-B

122

KAYSVILLE

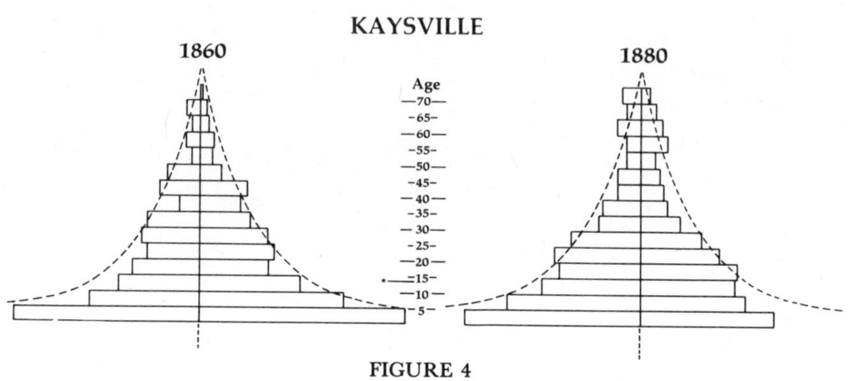

FIGURE 4

SPRINGVILLE

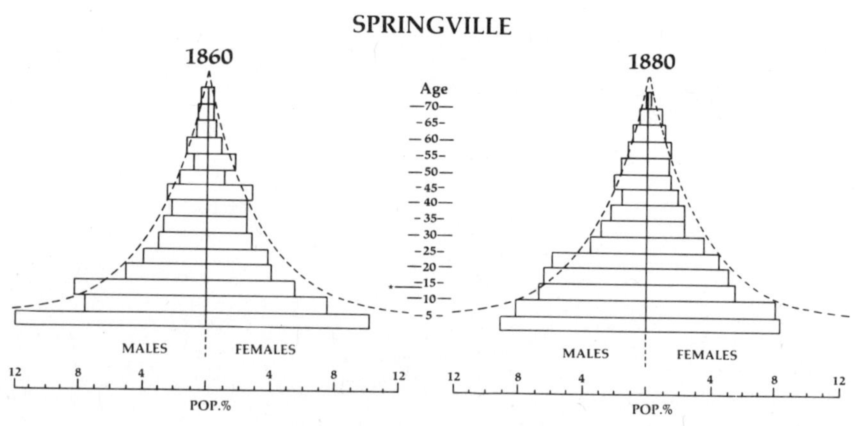

*Age 14 and above: Too old to have been Utah born

WEBER STATE COLLEGE CARTOGRAPHIC LAB

FIGURE 5

ty-five years of age. The high proportion of children becomes a little more understandable when one examines the sex distribution at various ages. Between fifteen and forty years of age (the major child-bearing years) females comprised 18.3 percent of the population, while males accounted for 12.8 percent. The actual numbers were 123 males and 177 females. By 1880 the proportion of children under ten had dropped from 42 percent to 31.3 percent while the proportion of people between the ages of fifteen and forty years of age increased from 28.1 percent to 33.1 percent. Females still outnumbered males (three to two) between twenty and forty-five years of age.

The basic age and sex structure of the populaion of Kaysville and Springville was similar to that of Brigham City. The proportion of young children was not quite as high and the population was a little more evenly distributed between the sexes. But the youthful nature of the population is immediately apparent. By 1880 the population was maturing. The proportion of children under ten had dropped significantly, while the other age groups had increased. The greater maturity of the population was evidenced by the increase in the proportion of people over forty-five years of age. It increased from 8.6 percent to 13.2 percent in Kaysville and from 10.7 percent to 12.8 percent in Springville.

A summary table of age and sex data for twelve selected towns and cities along the Wasatch Front makes several generalizations possible:

1. The ratio of males to females remained relatively stable throughout the twenty year period, with the mean ratio varying only 2 percentage points.

2. The average population for the twelve communities nearly doubled between 1860 and 1870 but increased only slightly during the following decade. Salt Lake City, Ogden, and those communities in between (Bountiful and Farmington) grew more rapidly during the decade of the '70s than did those communities in Utah County—no doubt a reflection of the greater impact of the railroad on the northern communities.

3. The percentage of the population under fifteen declined from 52 percent in 1860 to 44 percent in 1880. Only two communities—American Fork and Payson—experienced an increase in the percentage of children over two decades.

4. While the percentage of children under fifteen years of age was

124

declining, the average age was increasing. It rose from 19.37 years of age in 1860 to 23.0 years of age in 1880. Only one community, Payson, experienced a decline in the average age; this was due to its unusually high average age in 1860 (23.19). By 1880, Payson's average age was not distinguishable from that of other settlements. Perhaps the most significant fact about the average age is not that it was increasing throughout the years but that it remained as low as it did. When the average age of a population remains under tewnty-five, one can expect a continual population explosion, since the majority of population is either in or approaching the childbearing age.

Ethnicity

A significant proportion of Utah immigrants came from foreign countries, particularly Europe, where conversion to Mormonism was almost tantamount to migration to the United States. The call for new converts to move to America and a well-organized immigration system must have added to the appeal of Mormonism; thousands of new converts, especially from Great Britain and the Scandinavian countries, migrated to Utah. In the fall of 1859, under the direction of Brigham Young, a revolving fund, the Perpetual Emigrating Fund (PEF), was established to assist emigration. Donations to this fund were solicited throughout the Church. The original purpose was to help remaining refugees scattered through Missouri and Iowa to make the journey to Utah, but it soon became the primary means of assisting immigrants from Europe to migrate to Utah as well. PEF agents were established in most of the major port cities of Europe to organize immigrating companies and book passage to America for them.

Some European immigrants who were not converts to Mormonism took advantage of the Mormon organization and arranged to migrate under its auspices. These gentile immigrants tend to inflate the figures of Mormon foreign immigration shown in Table 5, but they probably made up a very small minority and may be included in the category of "Missionaries and Other." Of course it should not be assumed that the number of European Mormon immigrants arriving in the United States can be simply added to Utah's population figures. In 1883, Utah had a foreign population of 54,615, which is considerably less than the total of 78,225 who migrated to America as indicated in

TABLE 4

**SUMMARY OF AGE AND SEX DATA OF SELECTED TOWNS AND CITIES ALONG
THE WASATCH FRONT, 1860–1880, COMPILED
FROM THE 1870 MANUSCRIPT U.S. POPULATION CENSUS TABLES**

Towns	Percent Males			Percent Females			Total Population			Percent under 15			Mean Age	
	1860	1870	1880	1860	1870	1880	1860	1870	1880	1860	1870	1880	1860	1880
Alpine	41	51	40	59	49	60	135	208	319	56	51	39	18.6	27.6
Am. Fork[a]	56	50	49	44	50	51	695	1115	1825	52	52	57	19.6	20.4
Bountiful	48	50	46	52	50	54	866	1517	1617	48	49	44	20.3	21.0
Brigham City	50	50	46	50	50	54	975	1312	1877	58	49	47	17.4	22.7
Corinne[b]		65	46		35	54		777	277		23	43		26.9
Farmington	41	51	46	59	49	54	586	896	1073	50	49	42	17.39	23.2
Lehi	51	49	52	49	51	48	831	1058	1490	47	50	46	21.17	21.3
Ogden	56	47	53	44	53	47	1463	3190	5246	54	46	39	19.05	21.2
Payson	45	50	51	55	50	49	830	1432	1788	43	46	46	23.19	20.4
Provo	58	51	51	42	49	49	2030	2384	2432	53	50	41	19.31	23.2
Salt Lake	51	50	46	49	50	54	8190	12910	20768	50	47	39	20.38	24.7
Willard[c]	52	53	57	48	47	43	627	552	412	63	45	45	15.63	23.1
Mean	50	51	49	50	49	51	1564	3113	3348	52	46	44	19.87	23.0

Data for 1860 and 1880 are based on 10 percent random sample. 1870 data represents total population except Ogden and
Salt Lake City, which were also based on 10 percent random sample. Salt Lake City in 1880 based on 2 percent random
sample.

[a]American Fork is listed as Lake City in 1860.

[b]Corrine did not exist in 1860.

[c]Willard in 1860 includes all people utilizing the Willard Post Office. The census did not identify Willard City.

126

Table 5. New immigrants usually came into the United States at New Orleans and sailed up the Mississippi and Missouri rivers to Kanesville (Council Bluffs), Iowa. Here they were outfitted with ox teams and wagons or handcarts for their trek to the Great Basin. Some immigrants came via New York City and traveled by rail as far as Chicago, completing their journey to Kanesville by wagon. Others stopped to work for several months or even years in eastern states before migrating on to Utah. William Richardson, a Mormon convert from a coal-mining district of Northern England, serves as an example. He immigrated to the United States in 1857 but lacked sufficient funds to complete the trip to Utah, and worked for several years in various coal mines in Pennsylvania before continuing his journey. His diary account includes numerous references to other Mormon miners he met in nearly every mine where he worked, men who likewise were waiting to obtain sufficient funds to enable them to complete their migration to Utah.

TABLE 5

MORMON IMMIGRATION FROM ABROAD[a]

1848	754	1859–60	2,433	1873	2,537
1849	2,078	1861–62	5,556	1874	2,006
1850	1,612	1863	3,646	1875	1,523
1851	1,370	1864	2,697	1876	1,184
1852	760	1865	1,301	1877	1,532
1853	2,626	1866	3,335	1878	1,864
1854	3,167	1867	660	1879	1,514
1854½	500	1868	3,232	1879	1,780
1855	4.294	1868	3,232	1880	1,780
1856	3,583	1870	917	1882	1,775
1857	2,181	1871	1,500	1883	2,460
1858	none	1872	1,631		

Total 72,551

Missionaries and Others 5,674

Grand Total 78,225

[a]Robert W. Sloan, *Utah Gazetteer & Directory of Logan, Ogden, Provo and Salt Lake Cities for 1884* (Salt Lake City: Herald Printing & Pub. Co., 1884).

The bulk of these immigrants made their way to Utah, where they constituted a substantial portion of the adult population and added to the complex processes of acculturation that were taking place as a distinctive Mormon culture emerged. The foreign-born constituted about 32 percent of the total population in 1860, 38 percent in 1870, 30 percent in 1880, and 34 percent in 1890. These percentages hardly give an accurate picture, however, since nearly half of the population was under fifteen years of age and thus accounted for a substantial portion of the native-born. The 1880 census breaks the nativity of the population down into each age group. While the foreign-born comprised only 30 percent of the total population, they constituted 57 percent of those over twenty years of age and 68 percent of those over thirty years of age.

Nativity

Table 6 shows the place of birth for the residents of each of the twelve settlements identified in Figure 2. There was considerably more variation between settlements with respect to the nativity of the population than to the age and sex structure. The native-born comprised on the average 63.6 percent of the total population, but it varied from 57.2 percent in Alpine City to a high of 76.8 percent at Farmington.

Nevertheless, the most striking feature about the ratio of foreign-born to native-born was not variability among communities, but rather the uniformity. The native-born comprised approximately two-thirds of the population in nearly every community. Of these native-born, approximately two-thirds or more were born in Utah, which meant that most of them were under twenty-one years of age. The first settlers had only been in the valley for twenty-three years at the time of the 1870 U.S. census, and the bulk of the population much less than that. Consequently, a significant majority of the adult population in each community, except Corinne, consisted of foreign-born.

One might expect a rather uneven absorption of foreign immigrants among Utah settlements. There would be a natural tendency for new arrivals to collect in those communities where they had relatives or friends, or where employment opportunities were greatest. Since it would seem unlikely that these attractions would be equally distributed through all communities, one would expect that this selective process

TABLE 6

**SUMMARY OF NATIVITY CHARACTERISTICS FOR SELECTED SETTLEMENTS
ALONG THE WASATCH FRONT, COMPILED FROM
THE 1870 MANUSCRIPT U.S. POPULATION CENSUS SCHEDULE**

	United States			Europe										Other		
Town	Utah	Other	U.S. % of Tot. Pop.	British Isles	% of For.-Born	% of Tot. Pop.	Scand-inavia	% of For.-Born	% of Tot. Pop.	Other Europe	% of For.-Born	% of Tot. Pop.	Europe % of Total	Other	% of For.-Born	% of Tot. Pop.
Alpine City	100	19	57.2	69	86.3	33.2	19	12.5	9.1	0	0	0	42.3	1	1.3	.5
American Fork	579	98	60.7	372	77.8	33.4	39	8.7	3.5	7	1.6	.6	37.4	20	4.5	1.9
Bountiful	781	254	68.3	435	90.8	28.7	22	4.6	1.5	8	1.7	.5	30.7	14	2.9	1.0
Brigham City	663	153	62.6	178	35.9	13.6	297	59.9	22.6	10	2.0	.8	37.0	11	2.2	.4
Corinne	86	402	62.8	107	37.0	13.8	34	11.8	4.4	48	16.6	6.2	24.3	100	34.6	12.9
Farmington[b]	474	214	76.8	182	87.5	20.3	23	11.1	2.6	0	0	0	22.9	3	1.4	.3
Lehi	524	135	62.3	299	75.3	28.3	71	12.9	6.7	21	5.3	2.0	37.1	6	1.5	.6
Ogden[a]	1320	780	41.4	1010	92.6	31.7	30	2.8	.9	40	3.7	1.3	33.9	10	.9	.3
Payson	671	424	76.2	264	77.4	18.4	17	5.0	1.2	49	14.4	3.4	23.0	11	3.2	.8
Provo City	1249	482	72.6	451	69.4	18.9	149	22.6	6.3	26	4.0	1.1	26.3	27	4.1	1.1
Salt Lake[a]	6430	2170	62.3	3870	74.3	30.0	890	17.1	6.9	370	7.1	2.9	37.1	80	1.5	.6
Willard	240	89	59.6	177	79.4	32.1	1	.4	.2	12	5.4	2.2	34.4	33	14.8	6.0
Mean	1093	435	63.6	618	73.6	25.2	123	14.1	5.4	49	5.2	1.8	32.2	26	6.0	2.2

[a]Based on 10 percent random sample.

[b]First eight pages were missing.

would produce some communities comprised largely of American-born, others of British-born, and still others of Scandinavian-born residents. In the case of Corinne and Brigham city, such a natural selection seems to have occurred, but in the other ten Wasatch Front settlements the percentage of foreign-born and the nationality of the populace varied only slightly from the norm.

Greater insight into the process of assimilation of the foreign-born into the various Core settlements can be gained if one looks at the nationalities of these immigrants. Three-fourths of them came from the British Isles, which meant that there was no language barrier or other serious cultural difference separating them from New England Mormons. British immigrants probably constituted nearly half of the adult population of Utah. Thus there was no feeling of minority status, and one might expect them to be found in large numbers in all communities. They comprised three-fourths or more of the foreign-born in nine of the twelve communities shown in Table 4. The exceptions were Brigham City, where they constituted only 35.9 percent of the foreign-born; Corinne, 37.0 percent; and Provo City, 69.4 percent. The highest concentration was Bountiful with 90.8 percent.

Scandinavia was the other large contributor of Utah immigrants. The mean percentage of Scandinavians for all communities listed in Table 6 was 14.1 percent of the foreign population, but it varied from a high of 59.9 percent in Brigham City to a low of .4 percent in Willard, about 12 miles to the south, which had only one Scandinavian. Scandinavians comprised a small but significant minority in all of the other Wasatch Front communities. The greatest concentration in actual numbers was in Salt Lake City, where approximately 890 Scandinavians resided, but they accounted for only 17.1 percent of the foreign-born. It was Brigham City that emerged as a city of Scandinavians. Here they accounted for 59.9 percent of the foreign-born. Family and friendship ties, combined with a common language, seem to have been the prime factors attracting Scandinavian immigrants to Brigham City. On the other hand, the language barrier and minority status in other settlements acted as a deterrent to their dispersal throughout Mormon communities.

Twenty-year Analysis of Nativity Trends

A comparison table (Table 7) of nativity characteristics of the popu-

130

lation for the twelve selected Core communities was also constructed for the two decades 1860–1880. The results clearly indicate that the ratio of the population born in Utah steadily increased, while the percentage of those born elsewhere in the United States steadily declined. Certainly the immigration of U.S. citizens to Utah was not keeping up with the rate of natural increase. The percentage of foreign-born, on the other hand, remained relatively stable throughout the twenty-year period, indicating that the high rate of natural increase was matched by immigration from Europe. Scandinavians comprised an ever-increasing percentage of the foreign-born, while the percentage of those from the British Isles declined. Of the twelve communities analyzed, eight had a larger percentage of Scandinavians in 1880 than in 1870, and nine had a lower percentage of those from the British Isles for the same period. The British Isles still accounted for an average of 67 percent of the foreign-born in 1880 while Scandinavia accounted for 19 percent, making a total of 86 percent, which represented a 6 percent drop from 92 percent in 1860. Immigrants from elsewhere in Europe were increasing, although they still accounted for a negligible proportion of the total foreign-born.

Summary

The Mormon migration to Salt Lake Valley was a continual one as missionaries continued their efforts to spread the message of the restored gospel to various nations of the earth. Nevertheless, it was the displaced persons from Illinois and Missouri who formed the nucleus of the Utah settlements, and the heaviest immigration to Utah came during the first decade of 1847–1856. Substantial immigration to Utah continued throughout the decade of the '60s, although it fluctuated from year to year. By 1869, when the transcontinental railroad was completed, Utah's population was approximately 93,000. After the completion of the railroad there were no organized wagon trains crossing the plains, and records of those arriving in the territory were not maintained since each family arranged its own passage on the railroad. The backlog of those waiting to come had dissipated by this time, and the focus of Church officials was on domestic affairs in Utah. This resulted in a steady decline in Mormon immigration.

As with most migrations, it was largely young people, not bearded patriarchs, who emigrated to Utah. Consequently, a high percentage of

TABLE 7

SUMMARY OF NATIVITY CHARACTERISTICS OF SELECTED WASATCH FRONT COMMUNITIES
1860–1880
COMPILED FROM THE MANUSCRIPT U.S. POPULATION CENSUS SCHEDULES

Towns	% of population born in Utah			% of population born elsewhere in U.S.			% of population foreign-born			% of foreign-born from British Isles			% of foreign-born from Scandinavia		
	1860	1870	1880	1860	1870	1880	1860	1870	1880	1860	1870	1880	1860	1870	1880
Alpine	42	48	39	25	9	18	33	43	43	97	86	71	0	13	29
Am. Fork[a]	44	52	66	23	9	10	33	39	24	81	78	89	8	9	11
Bountiful	32	52	65	39	17	8	29	31	27	81	91	91	8	5	4
Brigham City	37	51	54	19	12	6	44	37	40	58	36	25	38	60	70
Corinne[b]		11	43		52	43		37	14		37	25		12	0
Farmington	36	53	64	33	24	15	31	23	21	95	88	77	5	11	9
Lehi	36	50	64	25	13	3	39	37	33	68	75	71	15	13	21
Ogden	35	41	47	37	24	20	28	35	33	74	93	71	17	3	16
Payson	17	47	58	57	29	18	26	24	24	80	77	66	4	5	20
Provo	41	52	59	39	20	11	20	28	30	76	69	58	12	23	28
Salt Lake	36	47	45	28	16	14	37	37	41	86	74	66	8	17	23
Willard[c]	39	43	62	26	16	17	33	41	21	95	79	100	5	0	0
Mean	36	46	56	31	20	15	32	34	29	81	74	67	11	14	19

1860 and 1880 data based on 10 percent random sample. 1870 data represents total population, except Ogden and Salt Lake City, which were also based on 10 percent random sample. Salt Lake City in 1880 based on 2 percent random sample.

[a]American Fork is listed as Lake City in 1860.

[b]Corinne did not exist in 1860.

[c]Willard in 1860 includes all people utilizing the Willard Post Office. The census did not identify Willard City.

the adult population was within childbearing ages. The large number of young adults, combined with polygamous marriages and with the stress Mormonism placed on large families, produced an unusually high birth rate and an age structure that was dominated by children. The high proportion of children would assure a continual high growth rate as these people reached the childbearing ages. It also meant that the provision of adequate food, shelter, and clothing, as well as schooling, must have taxed the abilities of the small working population.

A large proportion of Mormon converts migrating to Utah were Europeans from the United Kingdom of Great Britain and from Scandinavia. Immigrants from Great Britain, who made up the bulk of the foreign-born, were widely distributed throughout Mormon Core communities, generally comprising three-fourths or more of the foreign-born. In most Mormon communities those from the British Isles probably accounted for more than half of the adult population. The major exception to this rule was Brigham City, where Scandinavians comprised nearly 60 percent of the foreign-born, compared wih 36 percent from the British Isles. Apparently the early settlement in Brigham City of a significant number of Scandinavians acted as a magnet to attract other Scandinavian immigrants to the area. In addition to the attraction of relatives or friends, there was the advantage of a common language and common culture, whereas in other communities language acted as a barrier to acculturation. The British Isles and Scandinavian immigrants accounted for approximately 88 percent of the foreign-born in the Wasatch Front area; and while the Scandinavians were concentrated in Brigham City and Salt Lake City, some of them were found in virtually every community.

Over the twenty-year period from 1860 to 1880, the rate of growth by immigration almost kept pace with the high rate of natural increase. The foreign-born comprised 32 percent of the population in 1860, 34 percent in 1870, and 29 percent in 1880, while the percentage of the U.S. population born outside Utah dropped steadily from 31 percent in 1860 to 15 percent in 1880. Clearly the Utah immigrants were coming primarily from Europe rather than the eastern United States. During the same period the proportion of the foreign-born coming from Scandinavia increased from 11 percent in 1860 to 19 percent in 1880, while the percentage from the British Isles declined from 81 percent to 67 percent.

The oft-used argument that polygamy was necessary in Utah because of the surplus of women has little basis in fact. The ratio of males to females was approximately equal in most Utah communities, although some discrepancies in individual age cohorts existed. It is true that the proportion of women in Mormon settlements was high compared with other western communities, but it was lower than that of many eastern states.

In 1860 the average (mean) Mormon settler along the Wasatch Front was Caucasian, not quite twenty years of age, with British-born parents and several younger brothers and sisters. He would likely be looking forward to the arrival of additional relatives from the old country in one of the immigrant trains expected that year. Statistically, slightly over half of his peers would be females, and a few of his friends would be Scandinavians. Younger children would be much more numerous than he, with the most common age cohort being between zero and five years of age.

Notes

1. "Manuscript Histories of Pioneer Companies" vol. 1, p. 1, LDS Church Archives, Salt Lake City.

2. Linus P. Brockett, *Our Western Empire* (San Francisco: Prently Bettesan Co., 1882), p. 1184.

3. "Fourth General Epistle of the Presidency," *Frontier Guardian*, 2, no. 23 (December 11, 1850).

4. *Deseret News*, December 24, 1856, cited in B. H. Roberts, *A Comprehensive History of the Church of Jesus Christ of Latter-day Saints*, 6 vols. (Salt Lake City: Deseret News Press, 1930), 4:226.

5. Richard F. Burton, *The City of the Saints* (New York: Harper & Brothers, 1862), p. 293.

6. Ibid., pp. 293–95.

7. F. Y. Fox, "The Mormon Land System" (Ph.D. diss., Northwestern University, 1932), p. 78.

8. Brockett, *Our Western Empire*, p. 1184.

9. U.S. Department of Commerce, Bureau of Census, *Tenth Census of the United States, 1880: Mortality and Vital Statistics*, vol. 11, part 1, pp. 17–19.

10. Ibid., part 2, p. 61.

11. Compilation of Vital Statistics from the LDS Conference Report, April 1965, Membership Statistical File, LDS Church Archives.

12. Stanley S. Ivins, "Notes on Mormon Polygamy," *Western Humanities Review* (1956), p. 231.

13. Computed from U.S. Census population data, 1850–1890.

14. In comparison, the percentage of population under 15 years of age in Latin America today is 42 percent, in Africa 44 percent, in Asia 40 percent, in Europe 25 percent, and in the United States 29 percent. Only six countries—Togo, Iraq, Costa Rica, Rhodesia, Nicaragua, and Ecuador—reach 48 percent which was the mean for the 1870 Mormon communities. See "1972 World Population Data Sheet," Population Reference Bureau, Inc.

Mapping Mormons Across
the Modern West

Dean R. Louder and Lowell Bennion

Introduction

To judge from their recent mapping of religious denominations in the United States, the National Council of Churches (NCC) strongly suggests that Mormonism predominates only in Utah. Their map[1] colors brown every county in the state, but none outside of it, to indicate a Mormon majority among the Church-affiliated population. Compared with earlier attempts to delimit a "Mormon culture region," this map—if accepted at face value—would require the conclusion that the area of Mormon dominance has shrunk significantly since 1940.

To judge from recent issues of the *Church News*, the LDS leadership would strongly suggest that with Mormons now living in 78 different countries, a parochial Utah church has transcended state and national boundaries to become a world church. Given the hierarchy's constant concern with growth, many members have become convinced that Utah now has fewer Saints than California and will soon have fewer than Mexico. They probably expressed little surprise at the First Presidency's recent decision to convert Utah itself into a mission field for the first time. But how would they react if they read official Church reports which show that Utah still overshadows all other areas in membership?

These conflicting views have increased our natural curiosity about the actual, if always changing, location of the Latter-day Saints. A few years ago, questions arose as to what Church statistics—when mapped—would reveal about the dynamic distribution of Mormons. The desired data were found, but to make them mappable it was necessary to assign the Church's ward and stake units, which gather the statistics, to

136

state counties. Only for Utah, as the NCC discovered, could the Church provide a breakdown of its membership by county. Eventually, two sets of maps were generated to show the spread of the Saints since they first occupied the Salt Lake Valley. One set highlights the diffusion of the LDS faith through space and time as measured by the appearance of ward units in counties across the United States. The other depicts the current distribution of Mormons in the American West, in both absolute and relative terms. The analysis of both sets represents the latest in a series of attempts since 1940 to isolate and identify a Mormon region within a national context.

The Diffusion of LDS Wards

The development of The Church of Jesus Christ of Latter-day Saints, since its implantation in the Salt Lake Valley, can be classified into four general periods. These eras are suggested not only by changes in the Church's position within the American polity, but also by the spread of Mormonism within the country.[2]

1850–1890: The Struggle for Statehood and Organized Colonization

The first era featured a prolonged struggle for statehood, clearly dominated by Brigham Young, who claimed territory over twice the size of present-day Utah. He and his followers failed to occupy or hold much of their desired Deseret, but the extent of colonization beyond the Salt Lake Valley during this formative period was still considerable and long characterized by an apparent southward bias.[3]

By 1860 (Figure 1), wards had been organized in twelve areas which later became counties.[4] The spatial pattern is linear, stretching from Bear Lake to St. George, and is familiar to all who have traveled old U.S. Highway 91 or Interstate 15 across Utah. This axis marks the settled part of the so-called Mormon Corridor to Southern California and constitutes what Meinig has called the first tier of Mormon colonization.[5]

Ten years later (Figure 2) the number of counties encompassing LDS wards had almost doubled, as Saints moved over the borders into the southeastern sections of Idaho and Nevada and, more importantly, "behind" the Wasatch Mountains. There they laid out a second and higher tier of settlements served today by U.S. Highway 89.

By 1880 (Figure 3), shortly after the death of Brigham Young, a filling in of remaining Utah valleys and a northern extension focusing on Pocatello and other parts of Idaho's Snake River Plain occurred. A salient feature of this map, however, is the appearance of four prominent "outliers" of settlement in the Little Colorado, Upper Gila, and San Pedro regions of eastern Arizona and in the San Luis Valley south of Alamosa, Colorado. Expansion into Wyoming for the first time began with the formation of a ward at Evanston.

During the next decade the Snake River Plain remained a popular area for LDS colonists, as evidenced by the new wards established there (Figure 4). The "Four Corners" region shows Mormon colonies for the first time in 1890. Wards were also created in two other new and contrasting areas—in Mesa, Arizona, destined to become a key Mormon town in the twentieth century, and in the fertile Star Valley of western Wyoming, which has maintained its agricultural orientation to the present. Finally, as a direct consequence of the polygamy issue, "foreign colonies" took root just beyond the national border in both Canada and Mexico.

The resolution of the polygamy question and the granting of statehood marked the close of an era and ushered in a new phase of LDS settlement history. No longer was colonization centrally controlled and expansive. The new phase, which Cowan has labeled "Reaction and Controversy" because of the disputed seating of Utah Congressmen B. H. Roberts and Reed Smoot, strikes us as a period of settlement stabilization.

1890–1918: Stabilization of Settlement

In the absence of lands available for colonization and in view of Utah's more favorable status within the American union, the Saints finally settled down at the turn of the century. Their leaders seemed content to consolidate the existing LDS communities, perhaps expecting them to conform, as it were, to their newfound respectability. Compared to the settlement pattern of the preceding period, the three decades after 1890 witnessed little expansion. Only in the Uinta Basin—earlier set aside for the Utes—and in the Big Horn Basin of Wyoming around 1900, the Blue Mountain country of eastern Oregon before 1910, and the El Paso region prior to 1920, are exceptions found to this new inward orientation (Figures 5–7).

The radius of the circle within which about 65 percent of all Latter-

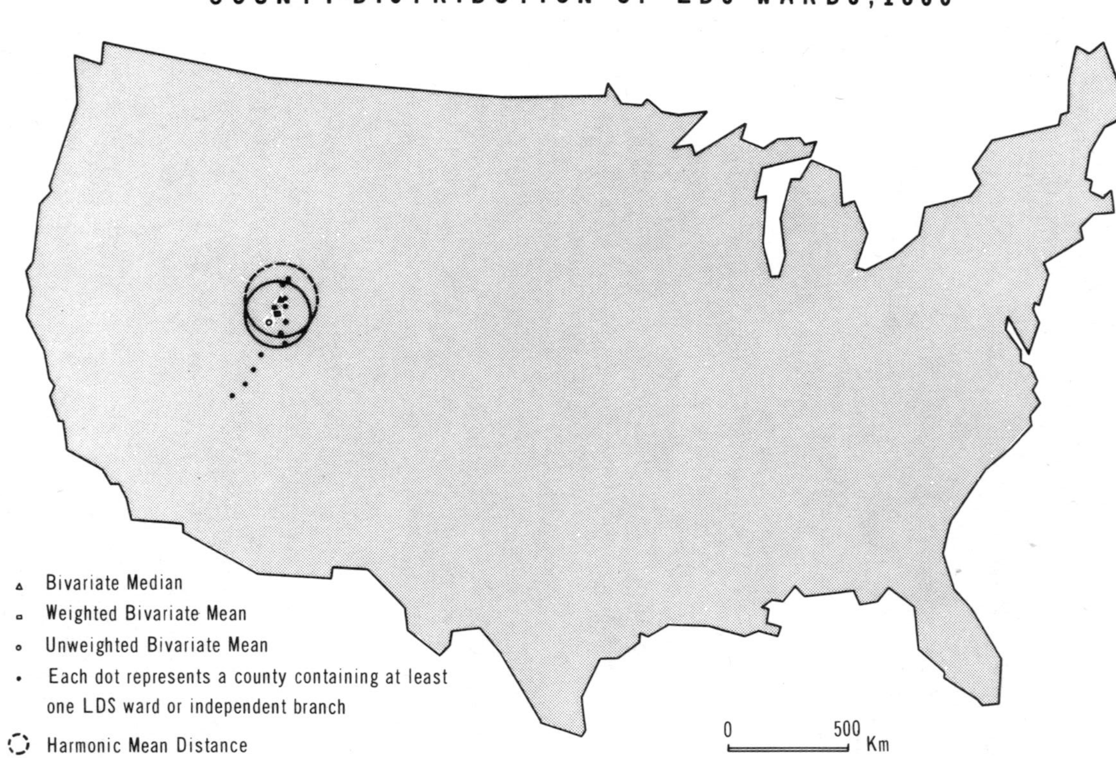

FIGURE 1

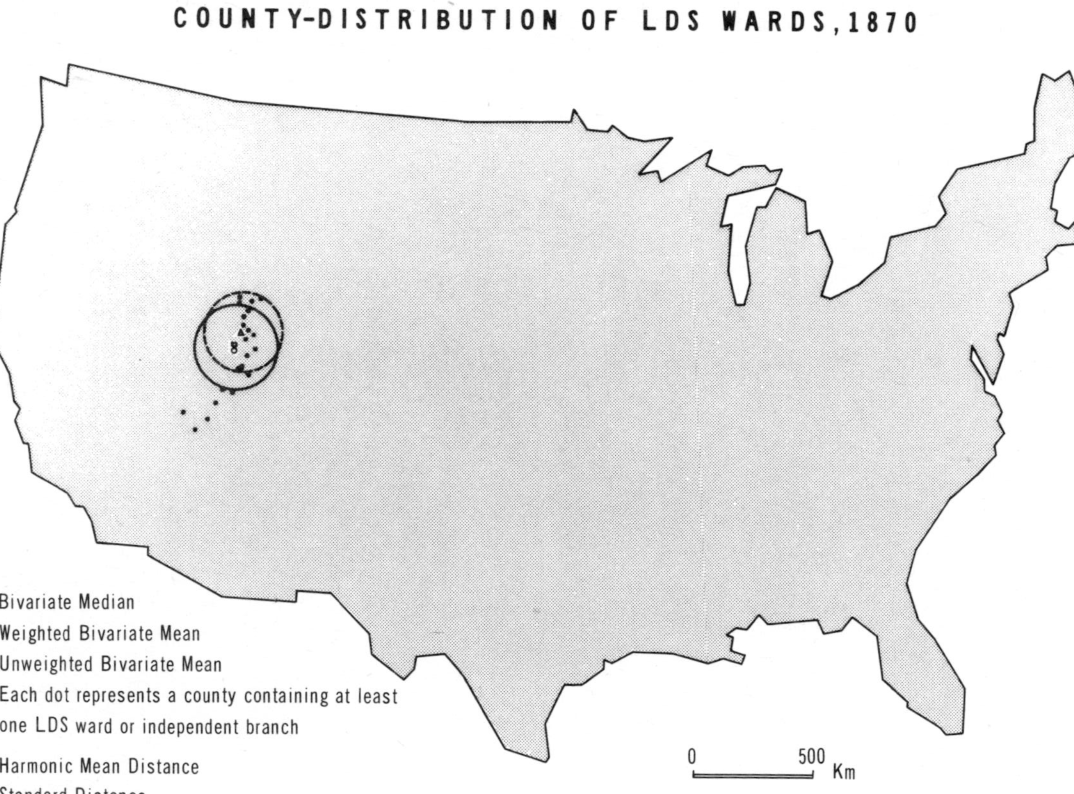

FIGURE 2

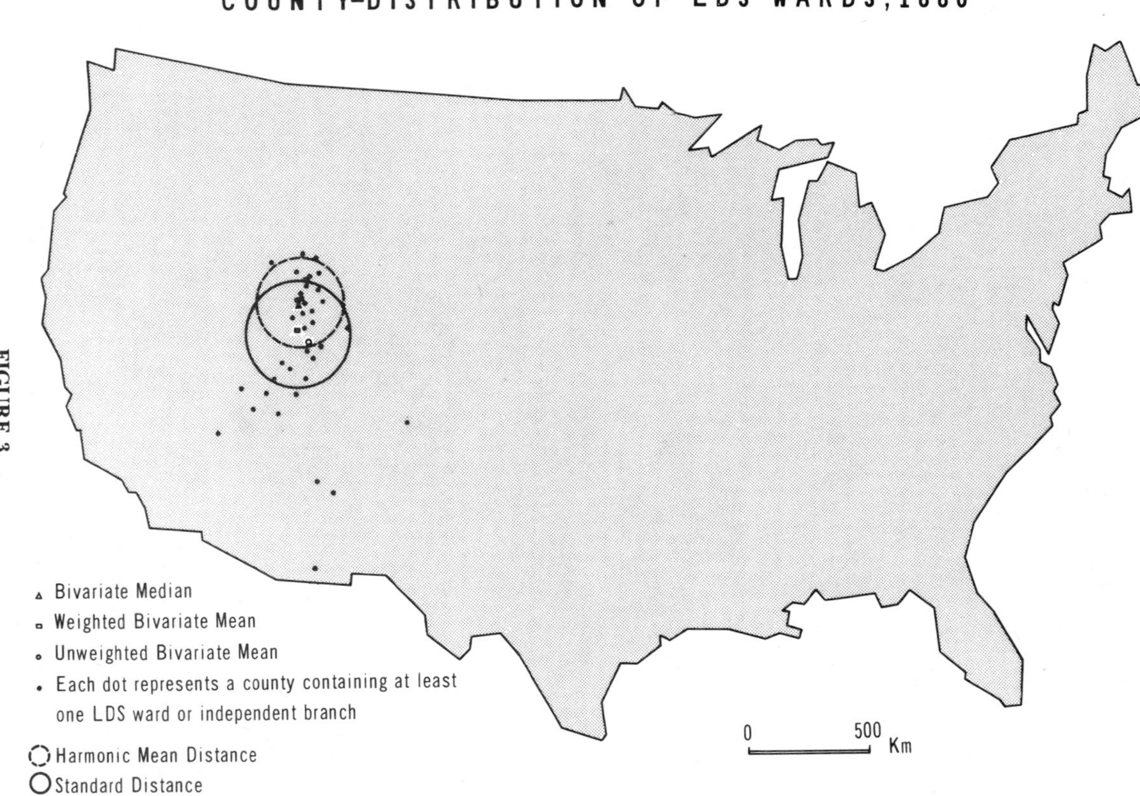

FIGURE 3

COUNTY-DISTRIBUTION OF LDS WARDS, 1890

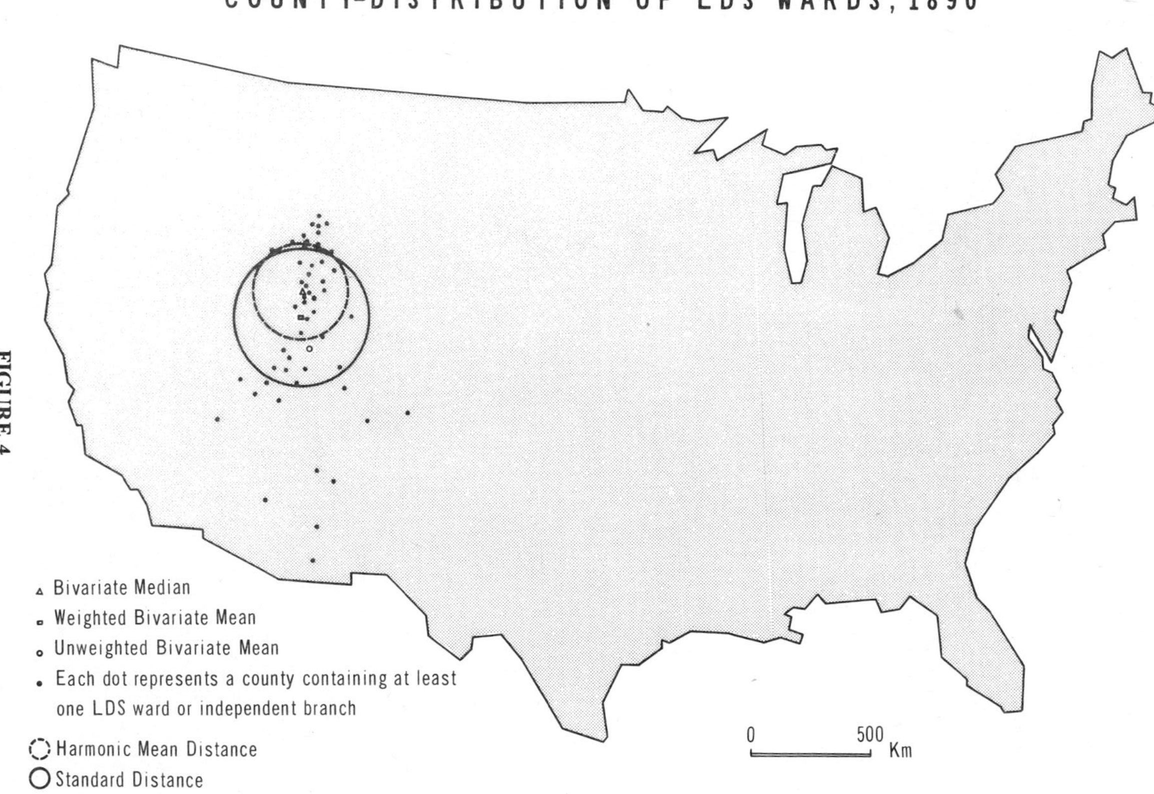

FIGURE 4

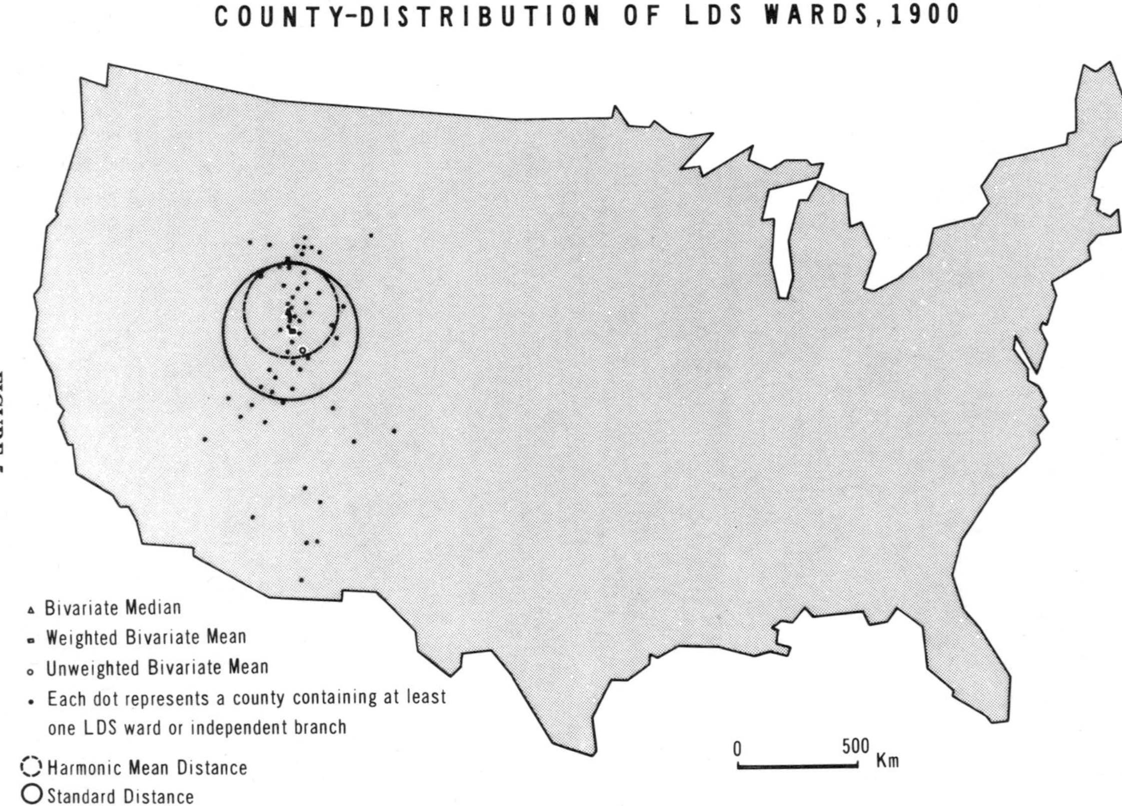

FIGURE 5

COUNTY-DISTRIBUTION OF LDS WARDS, 1910

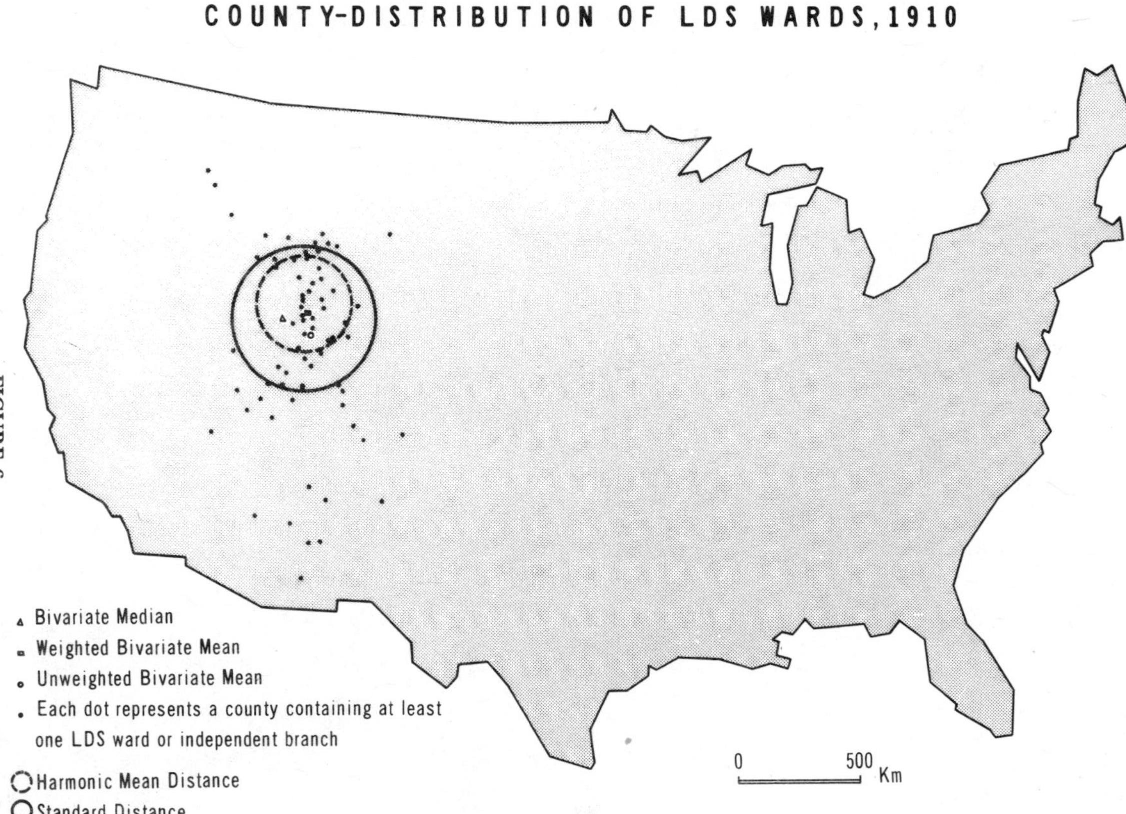

FIGURE 6

COUNTY-DISTRIBUTION OF LDS WARDS, 1920

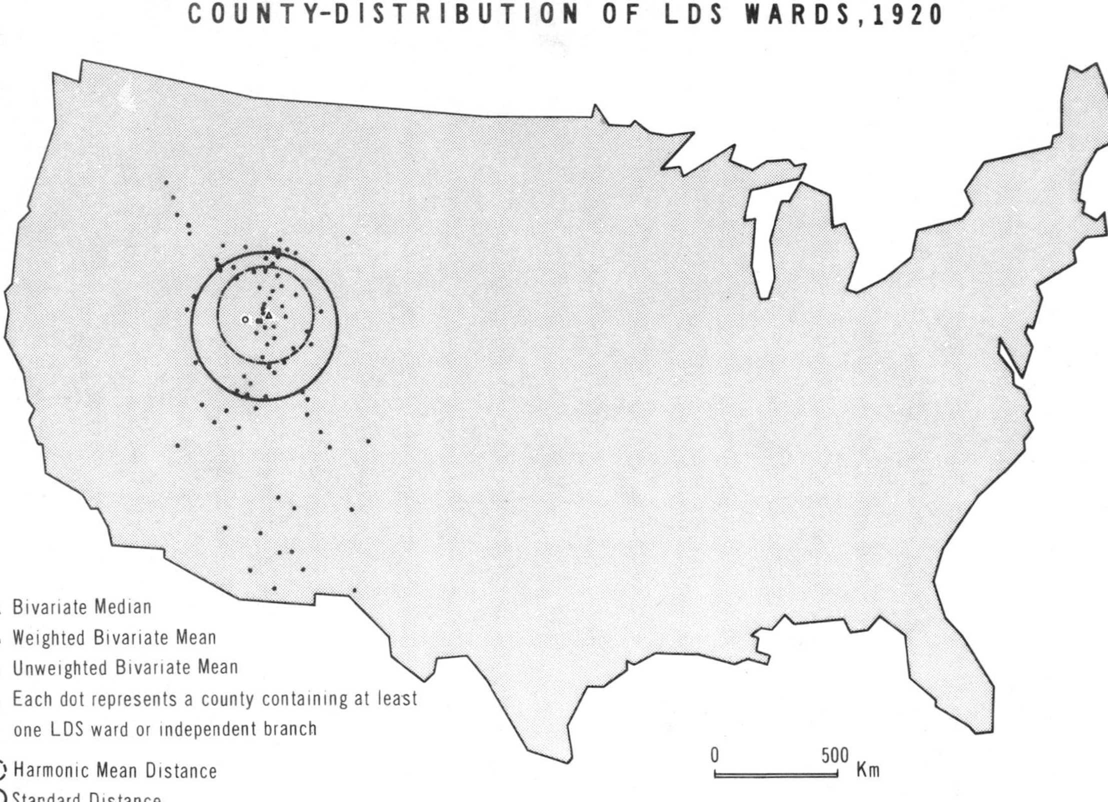

FIGURE 7

day Saints in the United States resided increased almost ninefold from 20 to 173 miles between 1850 and 1890.[6] But over the next three decades it increased only 16 miles. During this latter period, however, important policy changes were in the making which would alter the spatial distribution of the Mormon membership even more dramatically than the planned colonization of the nineteenth century.

The decisions to diminish the role of the Church in secular affairs and to terminate the "gathering" had become gospel by the beginning of the Heber J. Grant administration (1918–45). These decisions helped set in motion the events that led to the redistribution patterns observed in the third era, an epoch which Cowan has termed "Toward Acceptance," but which is designated in this paper as the period of West Coast expansion.

1918–1945: West Coast Expansion

The traditional centripetal forces which had bound Latter-day Saints to the Great Basin apparently weakened after World War I. As a result, many followed economic or other opportunities outside of the Mormon region, but largely to the burgeoning urban centers of western America. Evidently many Mormons still felt ill at ease in leaving Zion and striking out on their own in "Babylon." In 1921, for instance, Saints in Santa Monica, California, asked President Heber J. Grant "if living in California," a land so roundly condemned by Brigham Young in the past, "was out of harmony with Church policy." They received a reassuring but cautious reply: "At the present time the idea of a permanent settlement at Santa Monica is in full accordance with Church policies."[7] Soon after, in 1923, the Church reacted positively to the migration of members to California by establishing the first stake outside of the "Great Basin Kingdom" in Los Angeles. By 1930 (Figure 8), wards were visible not only in the Los Angeles area, but in San Diego and the Bay Area as well.

Even with the founding of wards and stakes in California, relatively few Mormons migrated to the Golden State prior to World War II. As of 1940 (Figure 9), the Church counted fewer than 50,000 members in the state. Even fewer lived in the other two Pacific Coast states, but they were also numerous enough there to justify the formation of wards and stakes.

The decade 1930–40 also witnessed the first full-fledged organization

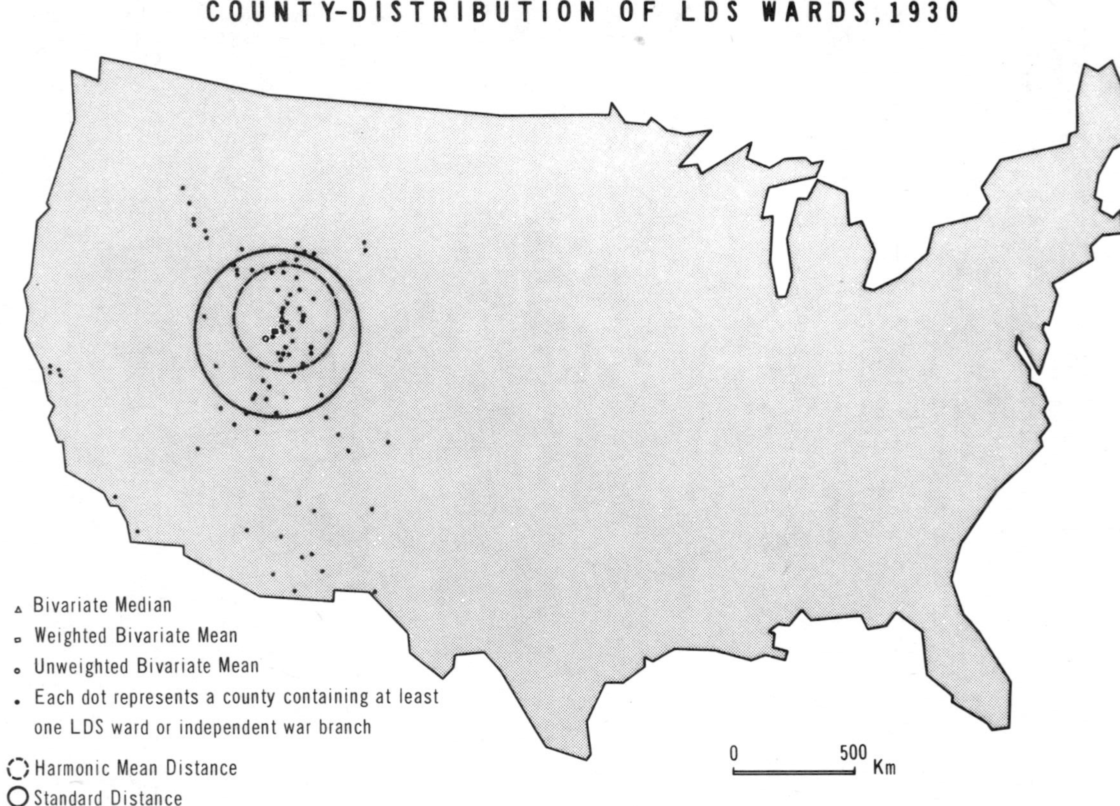

FIGURE 8

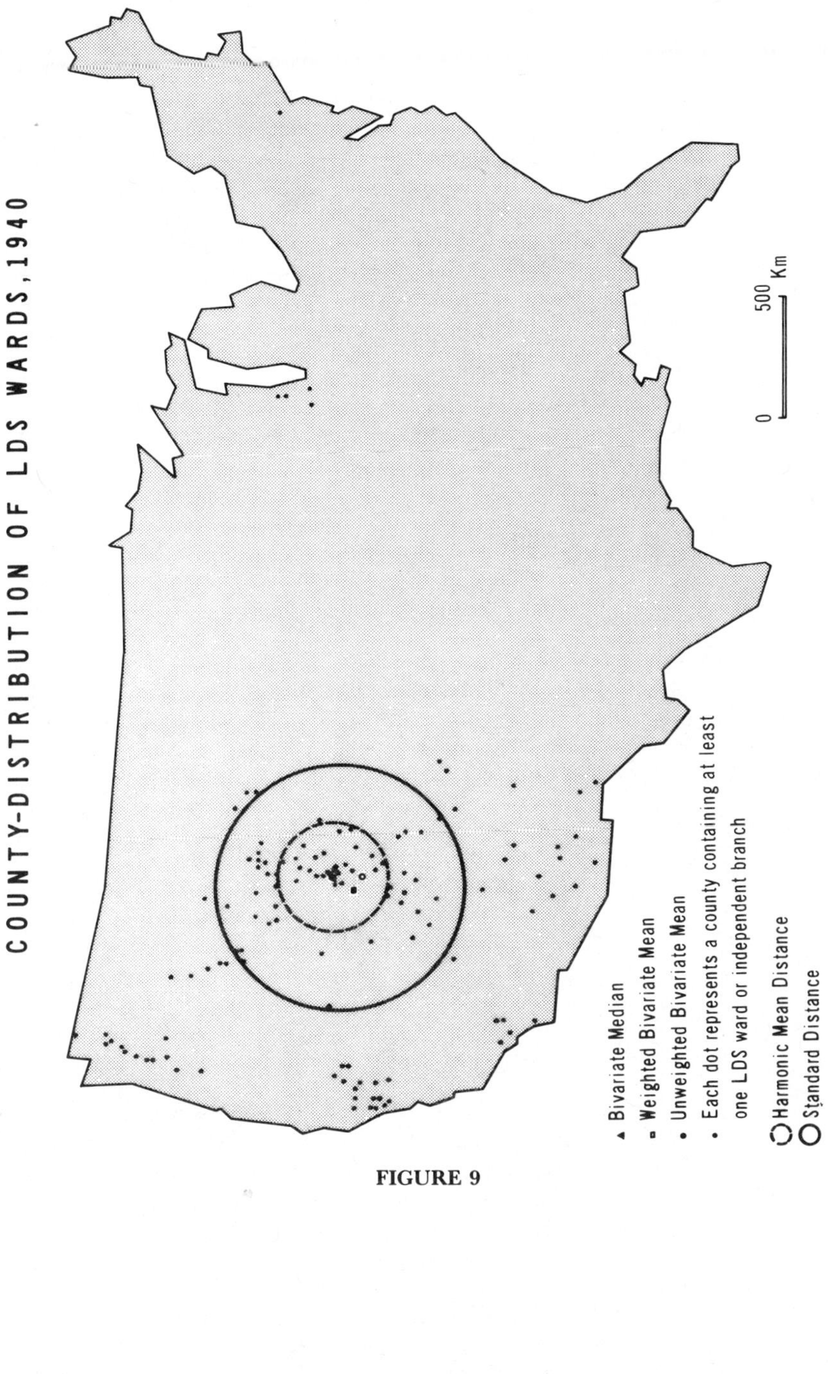

FIGURE 9

148

of the Church east of the Rockies—in the Chicago, Milwaukee, and New York metropolitan areas. These new units heralded the accelerated growth of the fourth era, when The Church of Jesus Christ of Latter-day Saints finally became, in the words of Cowan, a "Twentieth Century Denomination"—with a more nearly national distribution.

1945–1975: A National Denomination

The darkening in of the United States map by dots representing Mormon wards neared completion in this era, with large voids remaining only in Kentucky, Tennessee, and the Dakotas (all filled since 1970). The Church has become national, but only in the sense that it can now claim at least 1,000 members and two chapels in virtually every state of the Union.

A regional appellation for the first decade of the present period (Figure 10) might be the "Rise of the South."[8] Wards were organized most conspicuously in the Washington, D.C., and Baltimore areas, throughout the Carolinas, Georgia, and Florida, and in Texas. But they also sprung up elsewhere, as in the Pacific Northwest's Inland Empire, centered on Spokane.

By 1960 (Figure 11), wards had appeared throughout the South and had become ever more evident in the Midwest, notably in Indiana and Ohio. Expansion continued in Southern California, and for the first time formal Church organization took place in Montana (Figure 12).

Clearly the rapid postwar spread of the LDS Church into virgin territory cannot be explained solely in terms of declining secular influence within Zion and the slowing down of the gathering. The great missionary thrust of the past generation has played a major role. For example, approximately 42 percent of Church membership increase in the West must be attributed to conversions. In the Midwest the figure reaches 78 percent, and in the Northeast and the South slightly higher.[9]

It must be reiterated that each dot on the map represents merely one county containing at least one ward or independent branch. Thus a single dot may represent as many as 500 wards, as in Salt Lake County in 1970, or as few as one, as in the case of Cobb County, Georgia. Moreover, despite the rapid recent spread of the Church throughout the nation, in 1970 some 65 percent of all American Mormons continued to reside within about 700 miles of Salt Lake City.

COUNTY-DISTRIBUTION OF LDS WARDS, 1950

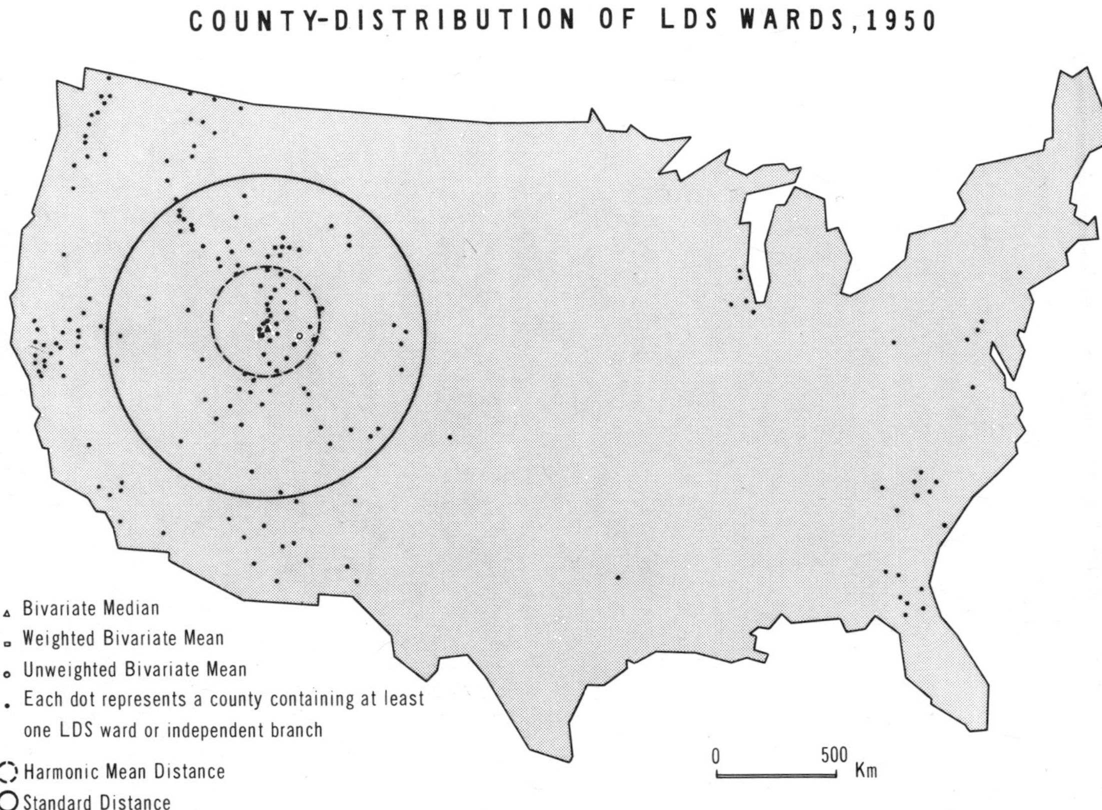

FIGURE 10

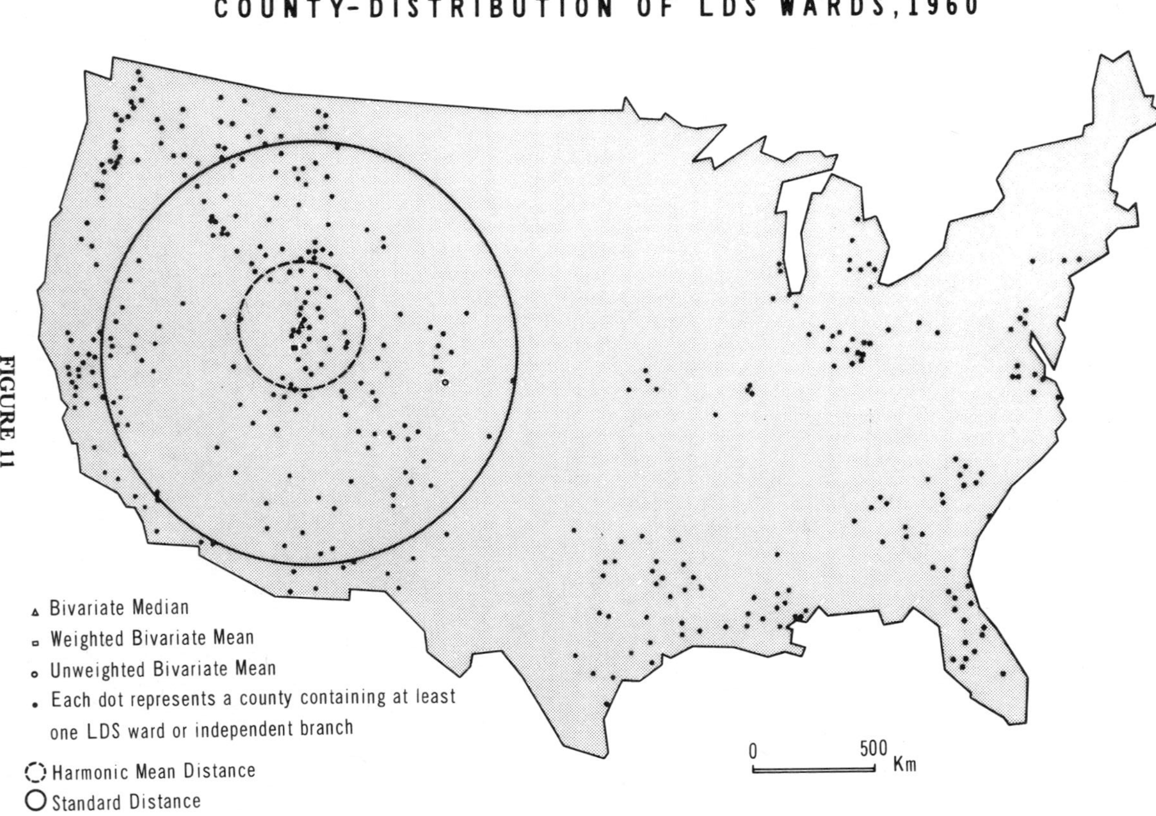

FIGURE 11

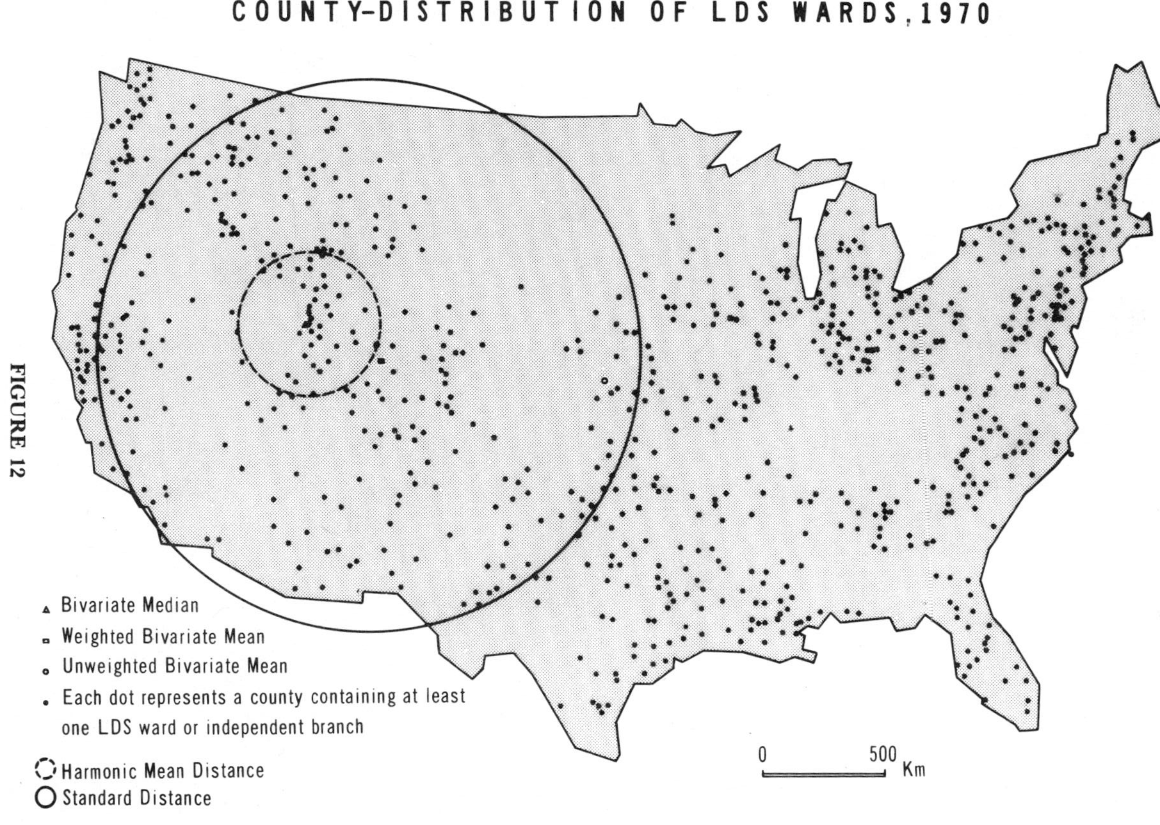

COUNTY-DISTRIBUTION OF LDS WARDS, 1970
FIGURE 12
Bivariate Median
Weighted Bivariate Mean
Unweighted Bivariate Mean
Each dot represents a county containing at least one LDS ward or independent branch
Harmonic Mean Distance
Standard Distance
0
500
Km

With the automobile and the mass media, they have easier access to Church headquarters than their parents or grandparents who lived much closer had. The geographical center of the LDS population in the United States only recently escaped Utah, moving just across the border into Colorado. Previously it had always lain within fifty miles of Salt Lake City (Figure 13). More than twice as many Saints still reside in Utah as in California. In fact, Utah accounts for more than one-third of the American members, and the national total (almost entirely English-speaking) accounts for roughly 70 percent of the world membership.

What in reality emerges at the national level is a gain in the relative proportion of Church membership on the West Coast at the expense of the Intermountain Region (Figure 14). Since 1920, all other regions have maintained a relatively constant and low percentage of the national total, the eastern United States representing barely a tithe of the total. Only in the Intermountain Region has the proportion declined, and only on the West Coast has it increased significantly. Given this strong western preponderance, with over 80 percent of all American Mormons residing within the eleven conterminous western states, it seems appropriate to examine their distribution in more detail.

The Mormon West

Since the 1930s, scholars in different disciplines have sought to identify homogenous culture areas within a heterogenous America.[10] Difficult as such an endeavor may seem, they have had little trouble in delineating a Mormon region because it is one of the few "regions whose religious distinctiveness is immediately apparent to the casual observer and is generally apprehended by their inhabitants."[11] We propose to compare this series of identified regions at the same scale for the first time. Then we will examine the present distribution of church membership to determine whether still another regionalization would be in order.

Recent Definitions

The very first versions of a Mormon region appeared in 1940, but they differed considerably in both name and shape. A. R. Mangus delineated a "Central Intermountain Region" as one of many rural regions of the United States. He employed such criteria as farm-village

CENTER OF GRAVITY OF L.D.S. WARDS IN THE UNITED STATES, 1860-1970

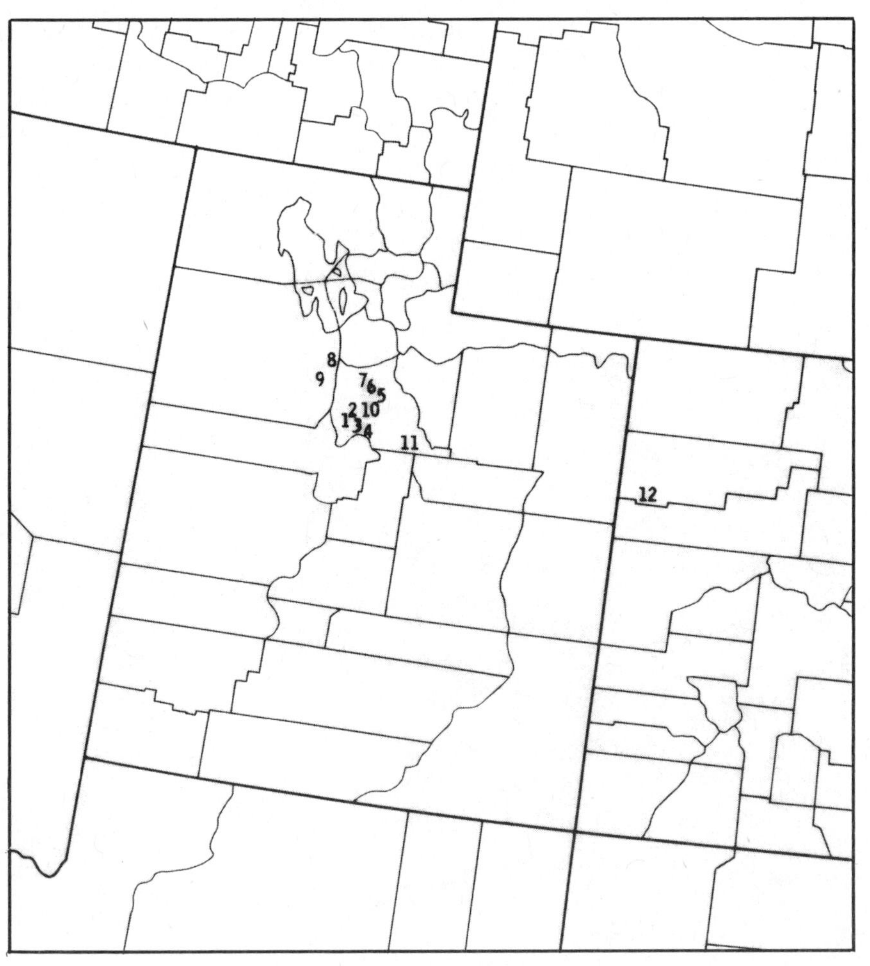

CENTER OF GRAVITY

1 : 1860	4 : 1890	7 : 1920	10 : 1950
2 : 1870	5 : 1900	8 : 1930	11 : 1960
3 : 1880	6 : 1910	9 : 1940	12 : 1970

FIGURE 13

REGIONAL COMPOSITION OF MEMBERSHIP, 1920–1970
CHURCH OF JESUS CHRIST OF LATTER–DAY SAINTS
NORTHEAST
ATLANTIC
GREAT LAKE
SOUTHEAST
NORTH CENTRAL
SOUTH CENTRAL
WEST
INTERMOUNTAIN
WEST COAST
% of total U.S. membership
500 miles
Source: Statistics compiled by Richard Cowan, Brigham Young University

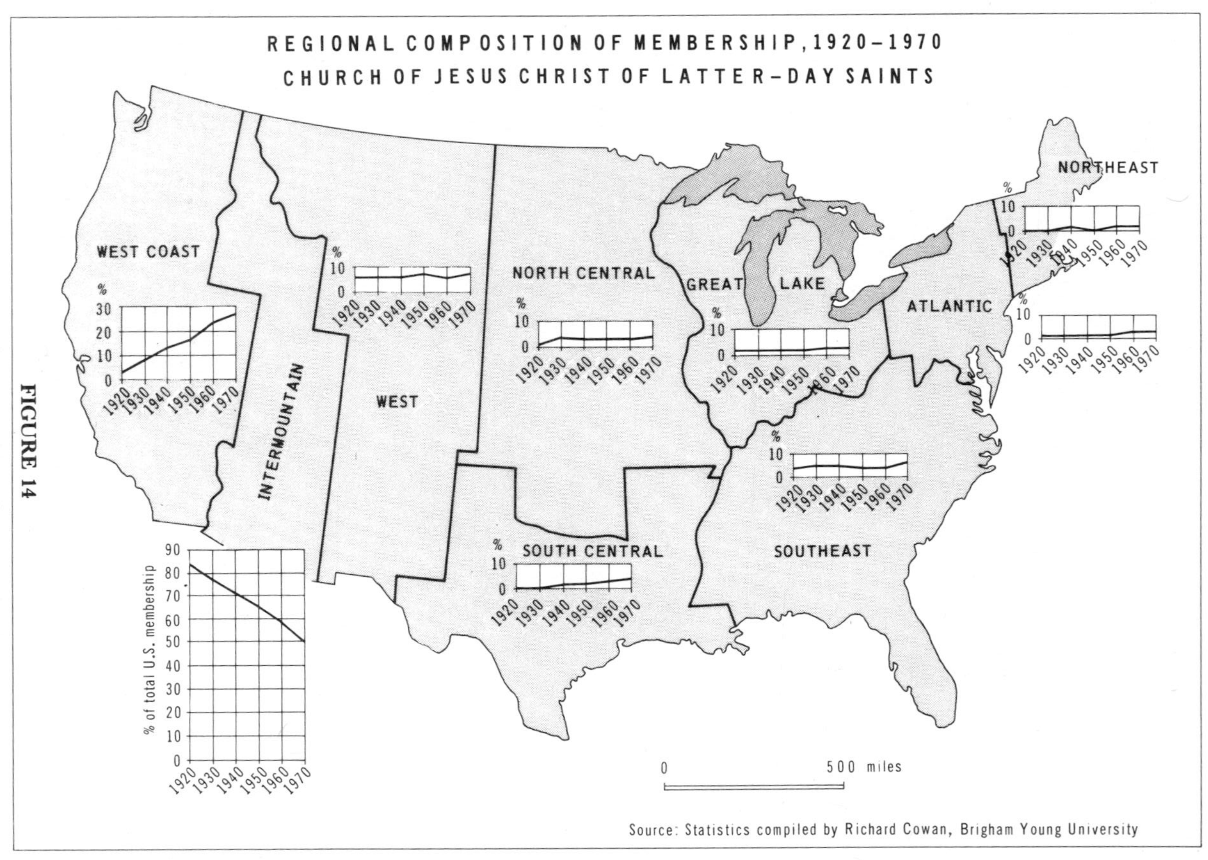

FIGURE 14

pattern, limited tenancy, and high fertility to derive his uniform region. Chauncy Harris, on the other hand, labeled his area the "Salt Lake Region" and derived it mainly from functional characteristics such as circulation networks focused on the Mormon capital. (See Figures 15 and 16.)[12]

A second and more similar pair of maps of a Mormon region was published in 1961–62 by Wilbur Zelinsky and Edwin Gaustad, who based their uniform version on the 1952 National Council of Churches' census, *Churches and Church Membership in the United States* (Figures 17 and 18).[13] Their use of the same data might have led one to expect an identical result, but along the edges their regions diverge noticeably. The differences may stem from the fact that Zelinsky depicted the Latter-day Saints as absolute numbers, whereas Gaustad portrayed them as a percentage of the total church-affiliated population in each county.

It remained for Donald Meinig to compare these two sets of definitions and then (in 1965) produce one of his own—what has become the standard version of "the Mormon Culture Region."[14] He combined, in effect, the functional approach emphasized by Harris with the uniform type of region constructed by the other three. Moreover, he added two new dimensions by examining the Mormon region in a historical context and by delimiting differences within it.

Meinig's regionalization posits a core, domain, and sphere (Figure 19). The *core* represents that nodal zone of high densities of distribution and intensities of interaction now known as the Wasatch Front. The *domain* designates areas of Utah and southeast Idaho that are dominated by Mormonism but where settlement is less dense and less integrated than in the core. The *sphere* signifies an outer zone of more dispersed distribution and more diffuse influence that reaches from the Boise Basin, around the domain, and across eastern Arizona into Chihuahua, Mexico. To include the tens of thousands of Mormons living in the major cities of the Far West, Meinig added a Pacific Coast metropolitan fringe to his map. He concluded that these Saints were not part of the sphere because they were recent, scattered migrants or converts whose location reflected national trends rather than LDS strategies.

Since 1965, R. V. Francaviglia has criticized Meinig for his failure to venture into the field and map distinctive features of the rural Mor-

M O R M O N   A R E A
(C.D. Harris, 1939)
0 - 1%
2 - 19%
20 - 49%
50 - 100%
PERCENTAGE OF TOTAL POPULATION BY COUNTIES

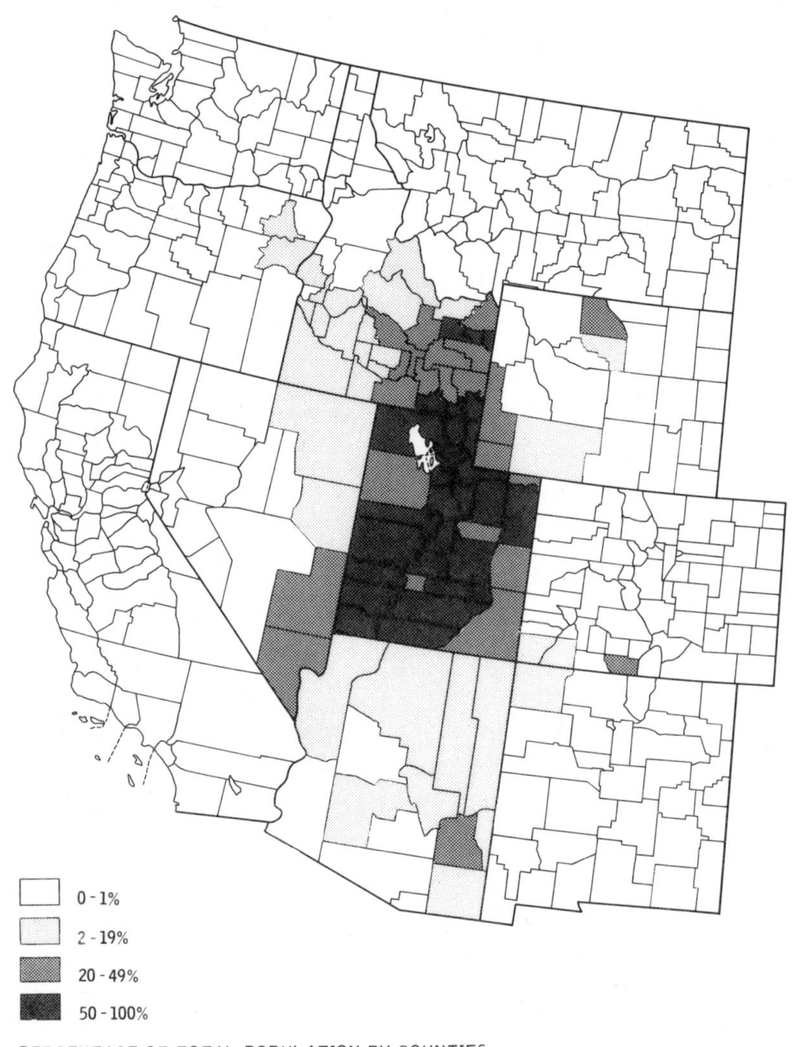

FIGURE 15

CENTRAL INTERMOUNTAIN REGION

(A.R. Mangus, 1940)

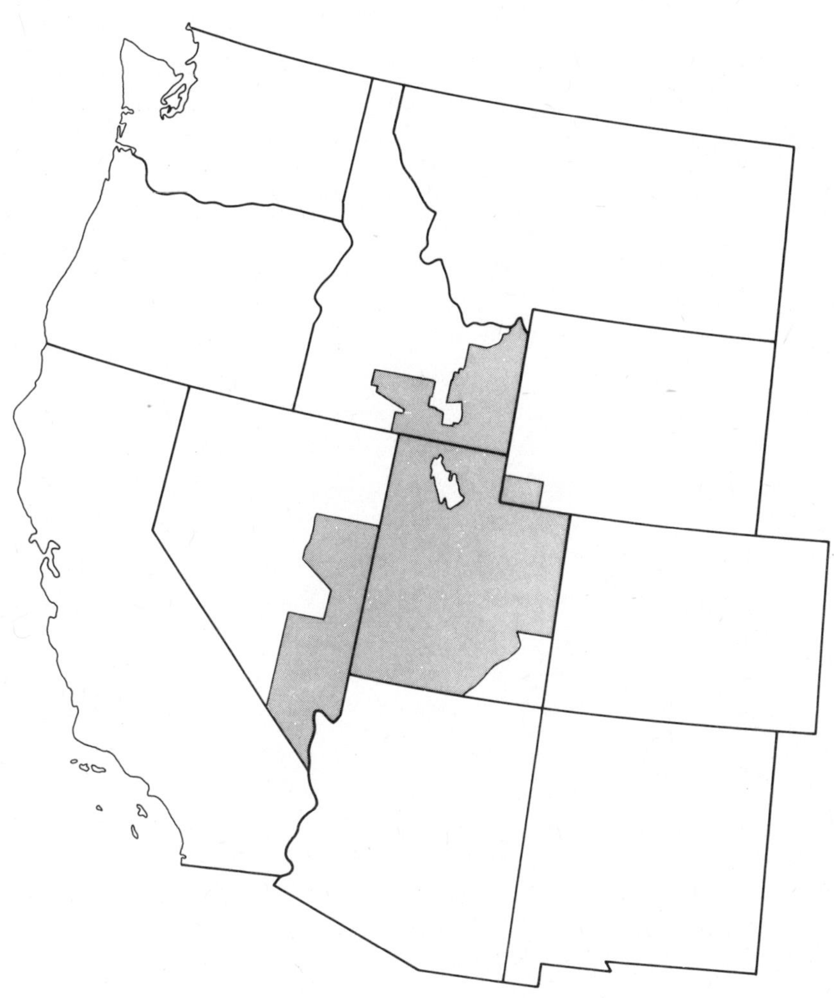

FIGURE 16

MORMON RELIGIOUS REGION
(W. Zelinsky, 1961)

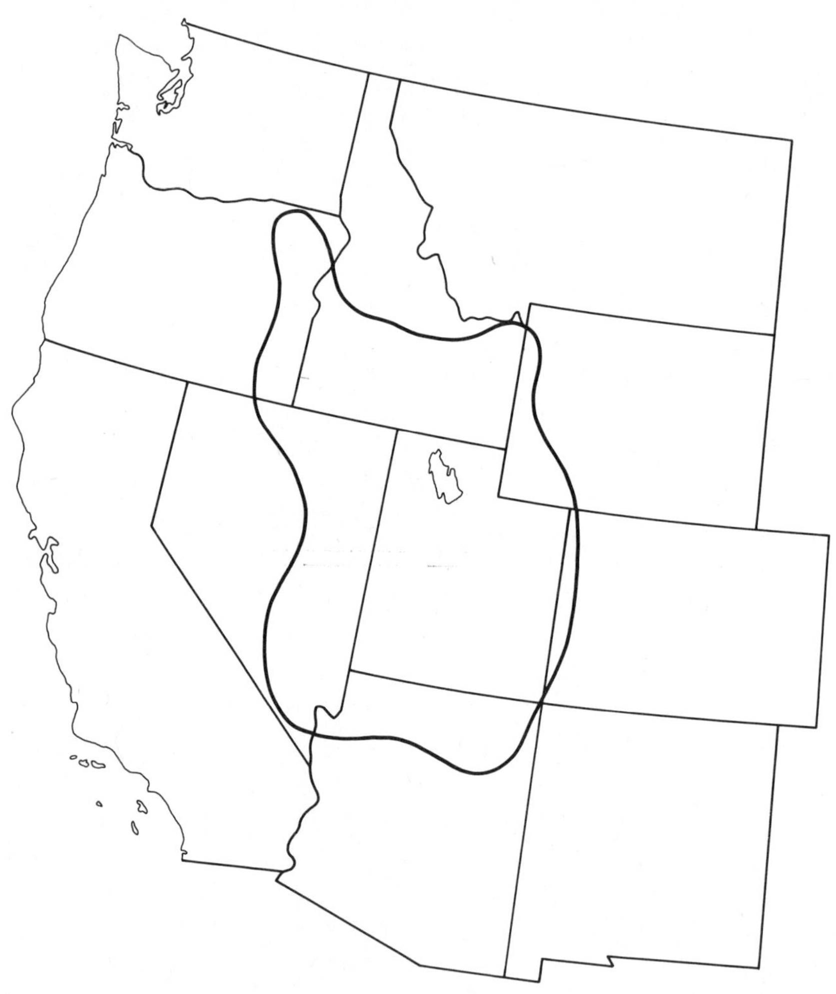

FIGURE 17

LATTER-DAY SAINT RELIGION IN AMERICA, 1950

(E.S. Gaustad, 1962)

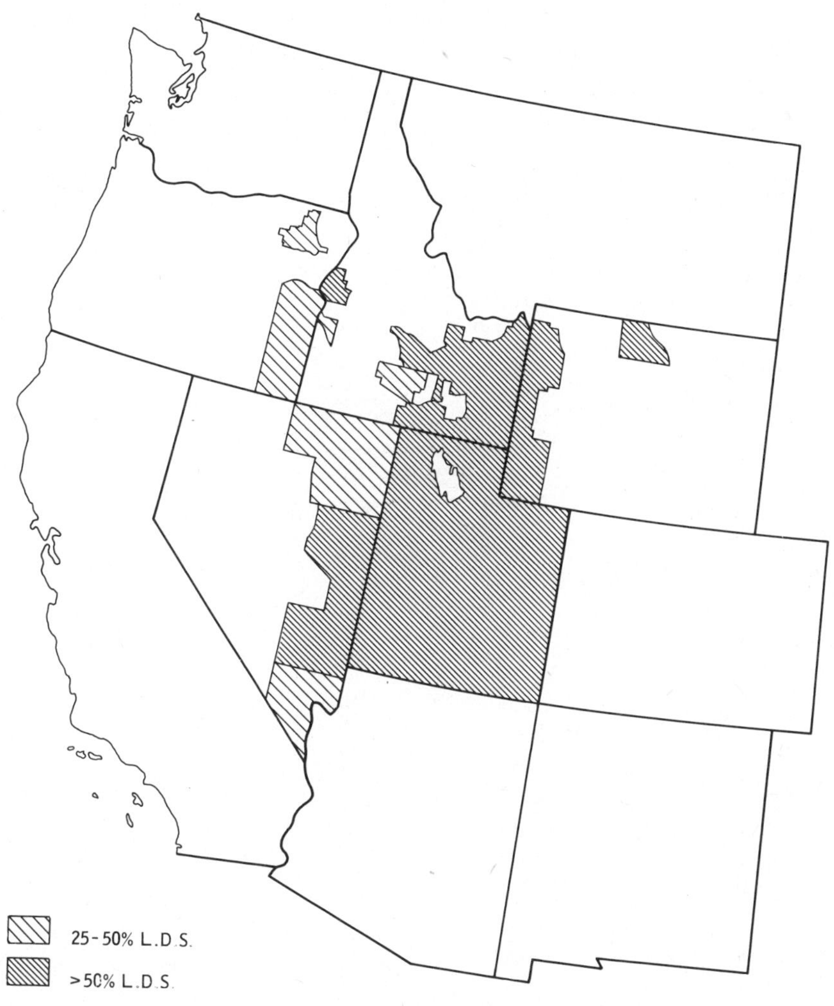

FIGURE 18

THE MORMON CULTURAL REGION
(D.W. Meinig, 1965)

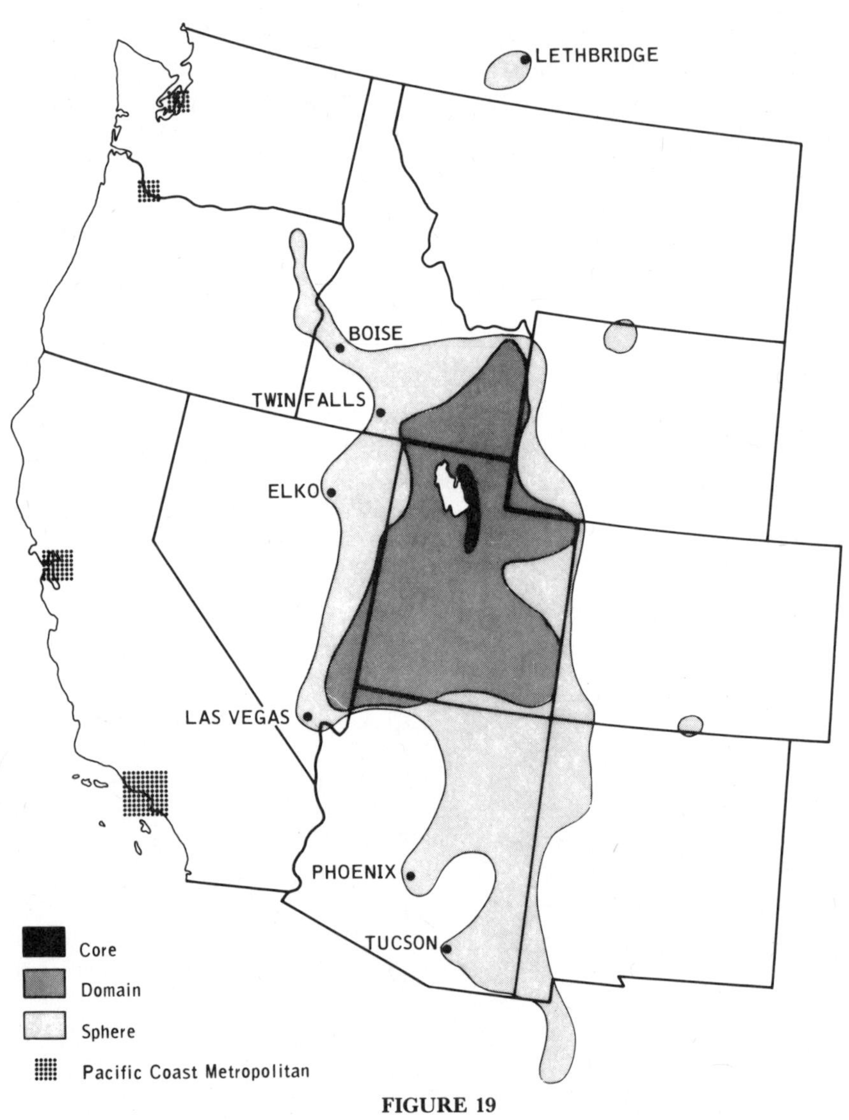

FIGURE 19

mon landscape that differentiate it from gentile areas.[15] Francaviglia himself tried to do this, singling out the following as key characteristics: wide streets, roadside irrigation ditches, barns and granaries in town, unpainted farm buildings, open fields around town, the hay derrick, the "Mormon fence," a domestic style of architecture, the predominant use of brick, and the ubiquitous ward chapels. He used the number of these elements observed in the landscape to devise and delimit another threefold version of a Mormon culture area consisting of a visual "nucleus," an "orb," and a "fringe" (Figure 20).

Overall, the superimposition of Francaviglia's map on Meinig's reveals little areal discordance. Significantly, however, much of the core on Figure 19 falls within the fringe on Figure 20, due to the intensive urbanization that has obliterated much of the traditional Mormon landscape. The arid reaches along the Utah-Nevada line which Meinig places in his sphere Francaviglia relegates to the non-Mormon West. If these latest delineations of a Mormon culture region are accepted as mutually reinforcing, it may prove instructive to compare them and the earlier versions with maps showing the current distribution of Latter-day Saints.

Present Distribution of Western Mormons

With the development since 1920 of a Mormon diaspora, the LDS Church has received requests from the media and politicians in western states for a county breakdown of membership data. In 1973 the Church Historical Department started responding to such inquiries by compiling Church statistics according to county for Arizona, Idaho, and California. Since then, with their assistance, the same thing has been done for the remaining western states, including Alaska and Hawaii, so that it has been possible to map and analyze the Church membership as absolute numbers (Figure 21) and as a percentage of the total population (Figure 22).[16]

Mapping western Mormons in these two ways proved relatively easy; comparing these maps with those already shown presented problems. None of the reproduced figures (Figures 15–19) directly compared with this pair.[17] Nevertheless, they provide an essential historical frame of reference for the analysis of the current configuration of Mormonism within the American West.

In absolute terms, several multicounty masses of Mormons immedi-

THE MORMON LANDSCAPE
(R.V. Francaviglia, 1970)

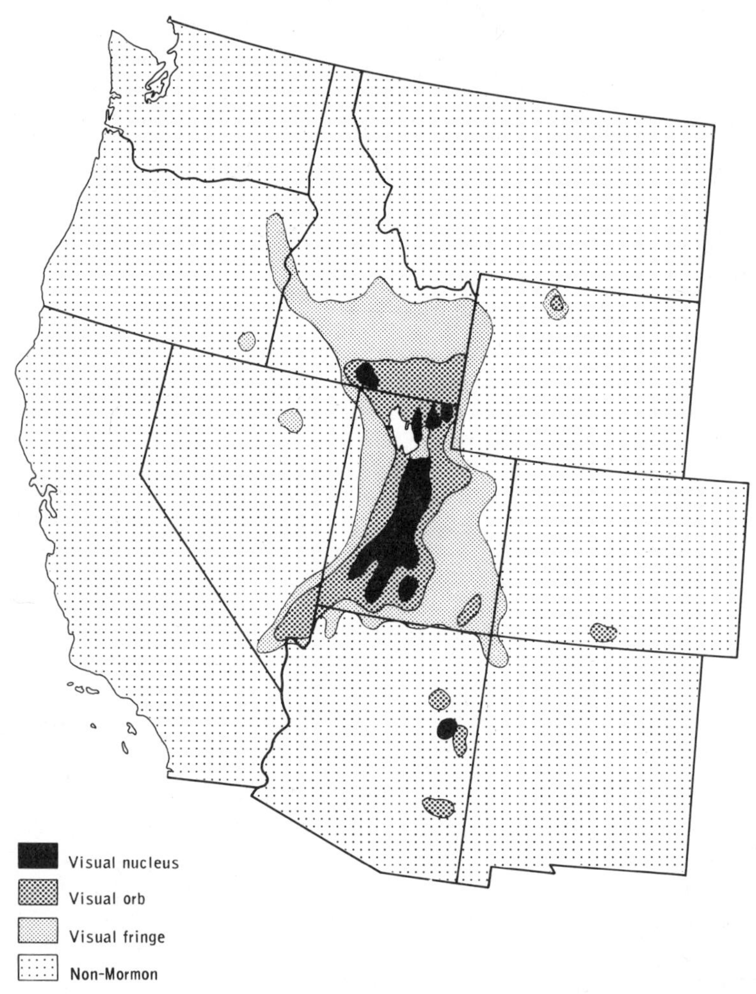

FIGURE 20

LATTER-DAY SAINT POPULATION, 1973
WESTERN UNITED STATES

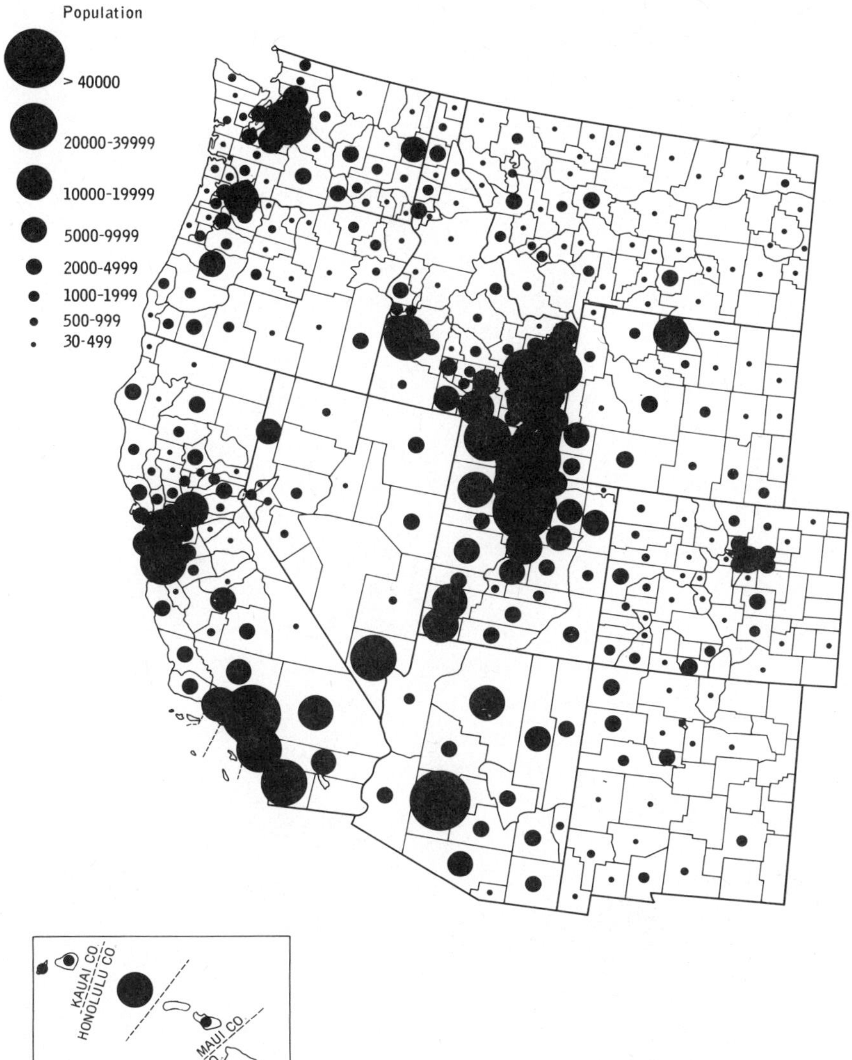

FIGURE 21

LATTER-DAY SAINT POPULATION AS A PERCENTAGE OF TOTAL POPULATION, 1973 WESTERN UNITED STATES

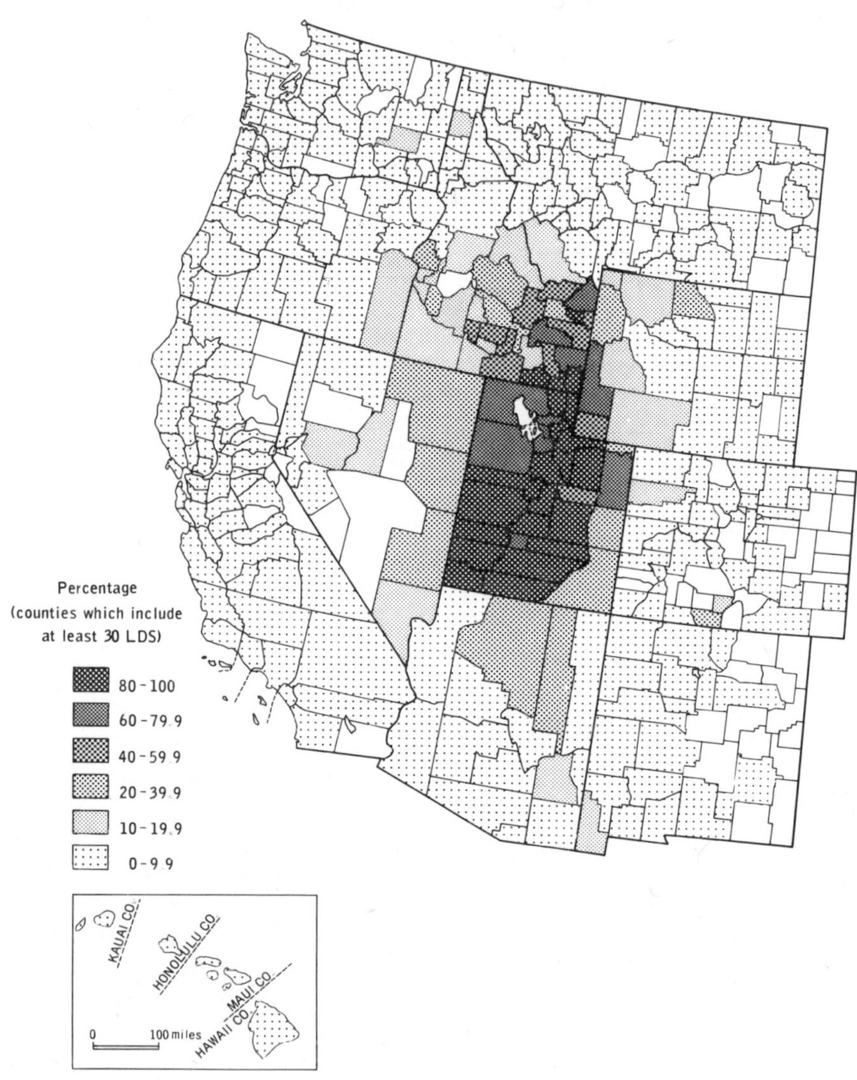

FIGURE 22

ately attract attention (Figure 21). Most dominant of all is the agglomeration along the Wasatch axis, with the four counties centered on Salt Lake City containing more than a half million members. The other major nodes tend to reflect the general distribution of population in the western United States, particularly along the Pacific Coast—from the Puget Sound (the logical location for the next temple in the U.S.) to Southern California. To Meinig's metropolitan centers would be added not only San Diego (with its new LDS Visitors Center) but also Phoenix, where many Mormons reside even though they comprise only about five percent of the total population. Outside of the four core area counties, only Maricopa (Phoenix) and Los Angeles number more than 40,000 members.

Along the eastern edge of the Rockies are found much smaller concentrations of Mormons, even in the most populous metropolitan areas. Denver is comparable in size to Phoenix but has only one-third as many Saints, fewer even than Las Vegas, which lies almost as far away from Salt lake City, but obviously benefits from its strategic location along the Salt Lake City—Los Angeles corridor. Similarly, the largest cities of Montana and New Mexico, particularly Santa Fe (with only one ward), have yet to develop many LDS congregations. Through and beyond the Rockies, the number of counties with few or no members increases quite markedly. The relative paucity of members at the eastern end of the western United States may indicate that the Mormon message still lacks widespread appeal among Americans of Mexican and Indian origin.

When the Church membership is mapped in relative terms, a somewhat different pattern emerges (Figure 22). The Wasatch axis remains dominant, but the absolute contrast between the Pacific Coast and the Rocky Mountain regions disappears. At first glance it may appear as if the percentage map reaffirms Meinig's model, but closer comparison suggests some subtle changes.

While the core and domain of Meinig's model retain their basic boundaries, the concentration of Mormons within them slowly but surely increases. The LDS percentage in Salt Lake City now approximates 70, and that in Utah as a whole 75, roughly 10 percent higher in both instances than a generation ago. This means that Saints are moving into the core-domain (and probably multiplying) faster than the gentiles as both converts and transplanted Utahns continue to pine

166

for Zion. Conversely, perhaps Mormons also leave the state at a slower rate. Only in three southeastern counties do Mormons remain a minority, and just barely so in the case of Carbon County. In southeast Idaho, Church members now constitute a majority in twelve counties, compared to six in 1930.[18]

The "intensification" tendency observed in the core and domain spills over into the sphere and beyond in all directions. Most of the counties in Meinig's sphere now have a larger Mormon minority than they did in 1930. Eastward, the most striking change has occurred in western Wyoming, bridging, in effect, the gap between Star Valley and the Big Horn Basin. The westernmost counties of both Colorado and New Mexico have experienced lesser but still significant increases in membership percentages, while the detached Mormon colony in the San Luis Valley of southern Colorado has more than held its own.

Westward the Mormon minority has also strengthened. In Nevada, all of the eastern counties except Clark have experienced a substantial percentage increase since 1930, and that pattern extends across central Nevada to the Washoe Front. More significant changes have taken place in southwest Idaho, where the Latter-day Saints have enhanced their position in and around both Boise and Twin Falls. Moreover, the appearance of sizeable Mormon minorities in southeast Washington almost suggests an extension of the Mormon sphere into the Columbia Basin. Whether these changes represent an influx of LDS migrants, or simply a reluctance of Mormons to leave an area, cannot be determined without more study at the local level. Whatever the reasons, the new patterns require a redrawing of the Mormon sphere, even if the only visible addition to the landscape has been the rise of a few more church spires.

Conclusions

What can be concluded from this general analysis of these two sets of maps? Clearly the LDS Church has acquired since 1918 an increasingly western and national configuration within the United States. This evolving pattern reflects the effects of policies instituted by President Heber J. Grant and the results of a greatly intensified missionary effort since World War II.

However, despite the force of these twentieth-century processes, the decisions made by Church leaders before 1918 continue to dominate the observed patterns of membership distribution. Mormonism remains very much rooted in Meinig's core and domain and, to a lesser degree, in an expanded version of his sphere. Indeed, in both absolute and relative terms, the LDS Church appears to be stronger than ever in its Great Basin Kingdom. Recent decisions to make all of this heartland—including Utah—an integral part of standard mission fields simply suggest a relentless quest for converts everywhere, even at home. The rest of the American West contains many members, but their distribution and influence are much more diffuse than in Zion.

To speak of a world Church is to express a hope and a goal that, from our spatial perspective, the Church cannot yet claim as a *fait accompli*. Even to speak of a truly national Church, one in which the Mormon percentage of the total population in the eastern states matches the national LDS average (about one percent in 1970), the Church will have to await more eastward migration from its western members and more successes from its missionaries, if not the Millennium itself.

168

Notes

1. The NCC's colored fold-out map accompanies D. W. Johnson et al., *Churches and Church Membership in the United States: An Enumeration by Region, State and County* (Washington, D.C.: Glenmary Research Center, 1974). Compare it with the maps of a Mormon culture region compiled by A. R. Mangus, *Rural Regions of the United States* (Washington: Work Projects Administration, 1940); C. D. Harris, *Salt Lake City, a Regional Capital* (Chicago, 1940); E. S. Gaustad, *Historical Atlas of Religion in America* (New York: Harper and Row, 1962); W. Zelinsky, "An Approach to the Religious Geography of the United States: Patterns of Church Membership in 1952," *Annals of the Association of American Geographers* 37(1961):139–70; D. W. Meinig, "The Mormon Culture Region: Strategies and Patterns in the Geography of the American West, 1847–1964," *Annals of the Association of American Geographers* 55(1965):191–221; and R. V. Francaviglia, "The Mormon Landscape: Definition of an Image in the American West," *Proceedings of the Association of American Geographers* 2(1970):59–61.

2. R. O. Cowan identified these periods, which we have adopted but modified slightly by means of a content analysis of the popular literture. See his "Mormonism in National Periodicals" (Ph.D. diss., Stanford University, 1961).

3. Meinig, *Mormon Culture*, p. 204.

4. For clarity of presentation only one dot is placed in each county, signifying the presence of *at least one* LDS ward or independent branch.

5. Meinig, *Mormon Culture*, pp. 201–2.

6. The circle, referred to in the literature of spatial statistics as the standard distance, is the bidimensional equivalent to the standard deviation in unidimensional statistics. Assuming a normal distribution, one standard distance encompasses 63 percent of the phenomenon studied compared to 68 percent for the standard deviation. For further details, see D. S. Neft, *Statistical Analysis of Areal Distributions* (Philadelphia: Regional Science Research Institute, 1966). To state that 65 percent of Latter-day Saints residing in the United States live within one standard distance of Salt Lake City assumes a relatively constant number of members per ward.

7. Quoted in Eugene E. Campbell, "A History of the Church of Jesus Christ of Latter-day Saints in California, 1846–1946" (Ph.D. diss., University of Southern California, 1952).

8. The history of the Church in the South goes back much further than the 1940s, however. It would be useful to know what retarded the formation of wards and stakes in this region for so long.

9. Dean R. Louder, "A Distributional and Diffusionary Analysis of the Mormon Church, 1850–1970" (Ph.D. diss., University of Washington, 1972).

10. See sources cited in reference 1.

11. Zelinsky, "Approach to Religious Geography," p. 165.

12. Mangus, *Rural Regions of the United States*, Figure 2; and Harris, *Salt Lake City, a Regional Capital*, Figure 18.

13. Zelinsky, "Approach to Religious Geography," Figure 26; and Gaustad, *Historical Atlas of Religion in America*, endpaper color map. An adapted version of Gaustad's map can be found in the *National Atlas of the United States of America* (Washington, D.C.: United States Department of the Interior, Geological Survey, 1970), p. 264.

14. Meinig, *Mormon Culture*, Figure 7.

15. Francaviglia, "Mormon Landscape," Map 1.

16. We owe special thanks to Gladys Noyce of the Church Historical Department and to William Allsop of the Membership Records Department for their assistance in converting Church membership statistics from ward and stake to county units. Since Mrs. Noyce had used 1973 figures for Arizona and Idaho, we used that year as our base date for all western states. We then divided the Church population by 1970 total population to obtain our Mormon percentages, which may therefore be skewed slightly by the three-year difference in dates.

17. Gaustad's map for 1952 may appear to be similar, but his use of church-affiliated population as a denominator yields a much higher percentage than total population would. Two maps that did not lend themselves to easy reproduction proved to be more directly comparable than the ones we have redrawn. Harris, *Salt Lake City, A Regional Capital*, computed the 1930 LDS percentage of the total population for the Great Basin Kingdom. Zelinsky, "Approach to Religious Geography," Figure 12, mapped the 1952 absolute distribution of all LDS, including members of the Reorganized Church.

18. See Harris, *Salt Lake City, a Regional Capital*, Figure 18, for this and subsequent comparisons with 1930 county percentages.